THE YOUNG CATHOLIC FAMILY
Religious Images and Marriage Fulfillment

by

Andrew M. Greeley

National Opinion Resear
and
University of Ariz

The Thomas More Press
Chicago, Illinois

D1472801

ISBN 0-88347-122-1

CONTENTS

THE YOUNG CATHOLIC FAMILY

Religious Images and Marriage Fulfillment

Introduction

Suppose that a writer is investigating the importance of religious images in the lives of adults -- the impact on their lives of the "imaginations" or "pictures" or "stories" which people carry around in their brains of various sacred realities. Suppose further that the author predicts on the basis of the conventional wisdom that we all know is true that such religious imagery can be expected to have little impact on, let us say, sexual fulfillment in marriage. And finally, let us assume that the author demonstrates empirically that his assumptions are correct. His efforts will receive little notice because, of course, he has merely sustained what everybody knows is true. In our secularized and secularist society, religious imagery is not very important. It may affect whether one goes to church on Sunday and even what one thinks in church on Sunday, but it can scarcely be expected to invade the bedroom and to affect what happens there. Why waste time, money, and energy to demonstrate that which is obviously true.

However, this monograph, based on an emerging theory of the sociology of religion, makes the exact opposite prediction. Religion and religious imagery will affect marital satisfaction and sexual fulfillment. Not only that, religious imagery will account for the substantial part of the ebb and flow of marital happiness in the first decade of marriage. Those young people who have "warm" or "passionate" images of sacred reality with "bounce back" more quickly from the doldrums which occur to many couples in the middle of the first decade of their marriage. Not only that, the religious imagery of a husband will affect the religious imagery of the wife and vice versa so that there is a propensity for a marriage to develop a joint religious imagery and it is precisely this development of a joint religious imagery which in part accounts for the "rebound" which occurs towards the end of the second decade of marriage.

Such assertions may seem theoretically implausible and almost certainly doomed to empirical falsification. "Everybody knows" that they couldn't possibly be true, not in secular, late twentieth century America.

Nonetheless, in the fourth chapter of the present work I propose to demonstrate that they are true and I will demonstrate their truth not as a part of a random exercise in computer sociology, but rather as a test of a detailed theory of the sociology of religion.

The data analyzed in this report were collected in the Knights of Columbus study of Catholic young adults. A little more than 400 of the young adults were married and questionnaires were sent to the spouses of these respondents. Approximately 80 percent of the spouses filled out these questionnaires, giving us a sample of 337 young Catholic families (a family in which at least one spouse is Catholic). The respondents represent a representative probability sample of self-identified Catholics in the United States between 18 and 30. Hence, the families are a representative sample of the families in which at least once spouse is a Catholic under 30 in the United States.

The principal aim of this report will be to analyze not individual respondents but family relationships. It should be noted that the costs of studying the young Catholic family are marginal given the fact that a study was already being done of young Catholic adults. The present report required only the money for printing, mailing and processing 400 extra questionnaires (and analyzing the data from these questionnaires and typing the present report). However, although the report cost practically nothing to produce, it must pay the price of being secondary analysis -- that is, analysis done with data which were collected for other purposes and hence not designed to specifically answer the questions with which this report is concerned. Only one extra question (no. 126) was added to the basic Knights of Columbus study questionnaire to facilitate this investigation. If one were designing a study of family relationships instead of a family of young adults, a much more detailed and elaborate set of questions would have been prepared.

Furthermore, while there exists no other data set in the country containing information on a representative national sample of young Catholic families, the data set on which this report is based contains a relatively limited number of cases. Hence, the analysis is necessarily delicate and intricate, particularly when one is attempting to falsify or verify subtle propositions from the sociology of religion. Most of the findings reported in this essay, however, are statistically significant (and are so indicated by an asterisk in the tables). Those which are not are advanced cautiously for whatever speculative use they might serve. At best, this report is a preliminary investigation into the impact of religious imagery on the lives of adults. But the beginning must be made somewhere, even with secondary analysis of a modestly sized data base.

I am not inclined, however, to apologize for secondary analysis of 337 cases. Let those who wish to be critical raise their own money, and do their own study of the young Catholic family.

In Chapter One I will present an overview of marriage adjustment among young Catholics. In Chapter Two I will turn to "joint" marital adjustment and analyze not individuals but family relationships. In Chapter Three, I will investigate the impact on these family relationships of religious behavior and in Chapter Four, the impact of religious imagery. Chapter Five will deal with the mini-life cycle of the twenties decade in which young people drift

away from the church and then return to it. It will show that family relationships and warm religious images account for much of the return. Chapters Six
and Seven (which will turn from family to individual data) will deal with
religious imagery's impact on social commitment, world view, and alienation.
Chapter Eight will describe the relationship between the "stories" of two
loves -- human and devine, and examine the question of what intimacy with
God and intimacy with one's spouse are linked to one another. In Chapter
Nine I will draw out those findings which seem to me to have particular
pertinence to theologians, pastoral workers, ecclesiastical administrators,
comment on the utility for religious practitioners of sophisticated
sociological theory and detail the urgent need for a lot more research on
the Catholic family.

I wish to acknowledge the help of my colleagues on the Knights of Columbus
project, William McCready, Joan Fee, and Teresa Sullivan, as well as the
enormous debt I owe for the development of my theories for the sociology
of religion to David Tracy and John Shea. I also wish to thank Virgil
Dechant, the head of the Knights of Columbus, his board, and the Knights as
an organization for their generous and enthusiastic support. Archbishop
Joseph L. Bernardin has been an enormous help in the project from beginning
to end.

OVERVIEW OF PRINCIPAL FINDINGS

1) A history of divorce affects negatively the satisfaction of a present marriage.

2) Mixed marriages are less satisfying, especially with the passage of time, since they rebound less dramatically from the crisis of the middle years of the first decade.

3) Similarly, invalid marriages are less likely to be satisfying than marriages at which a priest has officiated.

4) Finally, living together, because of its instability, is less likely to be a satisfying relationship, especially for men.

5) The marriages of Catholics who are not white are much less likely to be satisfying, presumably because of poverty.

6) Many marriages go through deterioration in the middle of the first decade and then rebound towards the end of the decade. Satisfaction in a marriage, both general and specifically sexual, takes a long time to build.

7) Children do not seem to impede the general satisfaction level of marriages, nor do they impede the sexual fulfillment save for those couples who have only one child during the middle years of the first decade of their marriage. For this group, sexual fulfillment seems virtually to collapse.

8) The average satisfaction level for women seems to be a result of the sexual fulfillment aspect of the marriage, particularly as perceived by their husbands. The decline in sexual fulfillment parallels a sharp decline in marital satisfaction for women and the resurgence of marital satisfaction in the last two years of the first decade for women is caused in part by a notable improvement in sexual fulfillment (as perceived by their husbands) of their marriage.

9) Thus, there is no confirmation at all why the pietistic position is taken by some Catholics that sexual fulfillment is not important to marriage satisfaction. It is very important indeed, especially for women.

10) The improvement of both sexual fulfillment and marriage satisfaction (as well as value consensus) between the eighth and the tenth year of marriage represents the decisive and critical turning point in the history of a marriage relationship in which many husbands and wives seem to be able to dramatically resolve some of the problems that effect their relationship and notably improve the quality of their married life.

11) About half of the young Catholic marriages were rated as "very satisfactory" by both partners. After a crisis for many marriages in the middle years of the first decade, some seven out of ten young Catholic families are described as "very satisfactory" by both husband and wife.

12) Sexual fulfillment, value consensus, and emotional satisfaction are the most powerful predictors of joint satisfaction with the marriage. Values and emotional satisfaction to some extent, and sexual fulfillment to a very considerable extent, go through a parallel life cycle decline and rise.

13) The proportion of young Catholic marriages which are jointly described as "excellent" in their sexual fulfillment doubles from the middle years to the last years in the first decade of marriage.

14) Sexual fulfillment in marriage is an extremely powerful predictor of whether a marriage goes into a decline in the middle years of the first decade and how deep that decline is.

15) There is no relationship at all between "liberal" attitudes on birth control, premarital sex, and living together, on the one hand, and marital satisfaction excellence and sexual fulfillment on the other. Neither is there any relationship between conservative attitudes on these issues and marital happiness.

16) The capacity to express love and to express disagreement does not relate directly to joint satisfaction with the quality of a marriage, but rather indirectly to their impact on value consensus and especially on sexual fulfillment.

17) Love, conflict, values, and sex seem to be the components of the dramatic crisis -- normally a crisis of growth -- which affects young Catholic marriages during the final years of their first decade.

18) Both the belief in life after death and church attendance -- when both spouses are involved in these attitudes and behavior -- lead to higher levels of marital fulfillment. The more religious a couple is, the happier they are in their marriage.

19) A sacramental marriage between two Catholics is also more satisfying and more fulfilling sexually than a mixed marriage. This satisfaction comes especially pronounced towards the end of the first decade of the marriage, as the sacramental marriage rebounds more vigorously from the crisis of the middle years of the first decade of marriage.

20) Religious devotion also facilitates the rebound of a marriage towards the end of the first decade both in terms of general satisfaction of both spouses with the relationship and also in their agreement that their sexuality and their value consensus are "excellent". The family that prays together may not stay together longer, but the family in which both husband and wife pray seems to improve the quality the longer it stays together.

21) Religious devotion influences marital satisfaction both directly and indirectly, the latter through its influence on sexual fulfillment and value consensus.

22) Family experience in childhood affects religious image of an adult and through that imagery marital happiness. The warmer the childhood, the "warmer" the religious imagery.

23) Warm religious imagery in turn affects both the capacity to express love and the capacity for sexual fulfillment. The warmer the religious imagery of husband and wife (as expressed in a joint measure), the more likely they are to describe a "warm" (i.e. "excellent") situation in their family with regard to both sexual fulfillment and capacity for loving.

24) In turn marital satisfaction (both "very satisfied") is to a considerable extent shaped by "warm" religious imagery and "warm" sexual fulfillment.

25) As a marriage develops, there are stronger correlations between the wife's religious imagery and the husband's religious imagery.

26) Much of the decline in sexual fulfillment and its subsequent rise are explainable by a model which takes into account family "warmth," religious "warmth," and the perceived capacity to love.

27) Much of the decline in marital satisfaction and its subsequent rise are explainable by a model which takes into account family "warmth," religious "warmth," the perceived quality to love, and sexual fulfillment.

28) Religious warmth and sexual fulfillment are the critical variables in the rebound of marriages at the end of their first decade.

29) Those who have intense religious experiences have warmer religious imagery and hence more satisfying marriages.

30) In both Canada and the United States, and in both English and French Canada, there is a religious life cycle during the 20's in which religous devotion declines and then rebounds.

31) The decline is the result of the alienation of young people from social structures in general, from the ecclesiastical structure in particular, and of disagreement between their sexual beliefs and the sexual teachings of the church.

32) This decline is effectively "cancelled out" by marriage, particularly in the United States by marriage to a Catholic.
Such a marriage leads to a decline in alienation and an increase in social integration and a diminishing support for sexual permissiveness.

33) Marriage to another Catholic leads to religious revival only if the spouses work out however implicitly a joint religious posture which emphasizes devotion.

34) In such marriages in particular, the joint religious imagery -- warm "stories" of God" -- play a decisive and critical role, diminishing alienation and cancelling permissiveness, and reinforcing the young Catholic's return to religious devotion.

On the basis of data available to us we cannot say that children make a contribution to the religious return of the late 20's. There is, in fact, no correlation between devotion and whether one has children or how many children one has. It is marriage, particularly marriage to a Catholic, rather than child-bearing and rearing, that accounts for the late 20's religious resurgence. It may be, however, that in the 30's the religious revival noted in Appendix C can be explained by the fact that during those years children reach an age at which it becomes necessary to hand on a religious tradition to them.

35) The process of religious reintegration that seems to go on in the late 20's, especially among those who are married to devout Catholic spouses, is intimately related to the process of religious reintegration. Just as the Catholic church is a net gainer in such reintegration, so is the Democratic Party; the latter because religious commitment seems to lead to social commitment and the Democratic Party apparently still appeals to young

36) Catholics as the party most likely to stand for social commitment. Warm images of God lead to warm political and social attitudes in young Catholic families where these images are shared by husband and wife. The more passionate one's stories of God, the more passionate one's involvement in the political and social work.

37) The religious life cycle does seem to be an actual life cycle phenomenon and not a generational difference.

38) There are "cold" as well as warm religious images; the former have the opposite effect on marital adjustment than the effect of the latter, correlating with low levels of sexual adjustment and marital satisfaction when both husband and wife are high on the "cold" scale. A combination of the sets of images explains a substantial proportion of the dramatic increase in marital adjustment at the end of the first decade of marriage.

39) The development of a warm religious imagination is in part the result of experiences -- a joyous family of origin, religious experiences, the experience of hearing good sermons, the experience of having a religious spouse, and the experience of traditional aesthetical practices. From the point of view of ecclesiastical policy making, a strong relationship between quality of sermons and warm religious imagery cannot be over-estimated.

40) Warm "stories of God" lead to a hopeful world view, a world view which, without denying the existence of evil, still sees goodness as stronger than evil (if on occasion only moderately so). Much of the influence of background experiences on hopefulness is filtered through warm religious images.

41) One may usefully conceptualize the impact of religious experience on the creative imagination by using St. Paul's terminology that "the spirit speaks to our spirit."

42) The hopefulness of one's world view, one's social commitment and one's propensity to frequent prayer are not influenced to any appreciable extent by one's doctrinal orthodoxy but strongly influenced by one's warm religious imagery.

43) Daily prayer by both spouses has an extraordinarily powerful relationship with sexual fulfillment. Those marriages in which both spouses pray every day are almost twice as likely to be marriages in which both spouses say their sexual fulfillment is excellent.

44) When daily prayer is added to warm family religious imagery (with which it correlates) almost three-quarters the rebound in family sexual fulfillment during the final years of the first decade of marriage can be explained.

45) Prayer, sexuality and religious imagery are intermittently interconnected. The relationship between the "stories" of two loves, human and divine, has been documented empirically for young Catholic families.

Chapter One - Individual Marital Happiness

There is no lack of evangelistic challenge for the American Church in the condition of the young Catholic family. Only a little better than half of the Catholics under thirty in the country (54 percent) are married to other Catholics. One percent have Jewish spouses, approximately one-third have Protestant spouses, and 13 percent are married to spouses with no religion at all. One third of the young Catholic adults were not married by a priest (and hence, canonically are "invalidly" married) and 18 percent are in "irregular" family situations. Ten percent are either divorced or separated and another 8 percent are living together out of wedlock (Tables 1.1 to 1.3).[1]

The proportion of Catholics marrying a person who was not raised in the Catholic religion does not represent a notable increase over the past. However, a decade ago approximately half of the non-Catholic spouses would have converted to Catholicism.* Hence, marriage conversions are much less likely now than they were then. The increase in mixed marriages seems to be more the result of the decline of the Church's efforts at marriage conversion than an increase in the selection of non-Catholics spouses (for a detailed discussion, see my Crisis In The Church, Thomas More Press, 1978.). However, the increase in invalid marriages for Catholic young people is striking as is the increase in living together out of wedlock. In another place, I will return to the analysis of these two phenomena.

Sixty-seven percent (Table 1.4) of young Catholic married people say that

---

[1]Tables 1 and 2 are based on the family data file, while Table 3 is based on the individual data file. However, there are no important differences in the proportion in invalid or mixed marriage between the two data files.

*Seventy-five percent of the respondents were born to "catholic" marriages, but presumably many of these marriages involved conversion (See Andrew Greeley, Crisis in the Church).

they are very satisfied with their marriage. Another 30 percent say they are moderately satisfied. Three percent say that they are not satisfied at all. In this analysis, we will lump the "moderately satisfied" and the "not satisfied at all" and consider them as a group which is something less than sufficiently happy in their marriage to say that they are "very satisfied". (Operating on the dictum of survey research folklore that one always moves down a response one category: "very satisfied" is taken not to imply complete and total satisfaction, a rarity in human relationships, but a tolerable balance of good things over bad things in a relationship; a "moderately satisfied" response indicates the balance between good and bad and the marriage is tending in the direction of the latter; "not satisfied at all" suggests that the marriage not only has serious problems but it is also in deep trouble.)

The distribution of young Catholics on the marital satisfaction question is not appreciably different from that of other young American adults of the same age. We are unable, however, to compare young Catholics with other young Americans on the marital "relationship" ratings presented in Table 1.5 since these ratings were designed explicitly for the present project. Only a minority rate their marriage as "excellent" on any of the ten items (wording of the entire question is to be found in Appendix A). Almost half say that their confidence and stability of their marriage is excellent and more than two-fifths consider their ability to express love and affection to be excellent, while a little under two-fifths say that basic value consensus is excellent. On most of the other "relationship ratings", approximately one-third evaluate their relationships as excellent though only about one-fifth think that religious agreement is excellent, and indeed, one-quarter describe their religious agreement as fair or poor.

(As we shall see subsequently, many of these "relationship ratings" vary through the years of marriage, going down in the middle of the decade and then going up towards the end of the first decade of marriage. But low satisfaction in religious agreement does not change -- even though there is a convergence in both religious behavior and religious imagery with the passage of time. Since religious agreement is not a high predictor of marital satisfaction -- in itself an interesting finding -- it is not analyzed in the present report but will be examined on another occasion.)

Men are more likely to consider themselves very satisfied in marriage than women (Table 1.6); whites more likely than non-whites; those who have not been divorced than those who were remarried after a divorce; those who are in all Catholic marriages and those who have been married by a priest as opposed to those who are in "mixed" or "invalid" marriages. The presence of children, a working wife, or a background of not being raised by both parents have no impact on marital satisfaction and while those who have gone to college are ten percentage points more likely to say that they are very happy, this relationship is not statistically significant.

It is worth emphasizing that the traditional Catholic opposition to mixed marriages and invalid marriages receive some confirmation in Table 1.6. There are lower levels of marital satisfaction for young Catholic in either mixed or invalid marriages than there are for those in valid Catholic marriages.

There are relatively few significant relationships between the background variables and the marital satisfaction rating items. Sexual fulfillment and emotional satisfaction are significantly higher for those who have no children and significantly lower for the non-white members of the Catholic population.[2]

---

[2]No detailed analysis attempted in this report of the marriages of "non-white" Catholics because there are not enough respondents in this category to be studied, nor are there enough divorced Catholics to be analyzed.

Thus, the principal question with which we are faced after inspection of Table 1.7 is why the presence of children in the families seems to affect the level of sexual fulfillment and emotional satisfaction in a marriage. ("Basic value agreement", "emotional satisfaction", and "sexual fulfillment" are chosen for analysis because they are the three variables which, as we will demonstrate subsequently, have the strongest predictive power in explaining marital satisfaction.)

Satisfaction with marriage is strongly related to the duration of the marriage (Table 1.8). Three-quarters of those who have been married less than two years say they are very satisfied. The proportion drops to about two-thirds for those who have been married between three and six years and to a little bit better than half (57%) for those who have been married seven or eight years. There is then a remarkable "rebound" to a 79 percent "very satisfied" response for those who have been married from nine to ten years. Interestingly enough, as noted in the preliminary Knights of Columbus report, there is a parallel decline and then rebound of religious practice among Catholics in their middle and late twenties.

Two possible dynamics may be at work in the data reported in Table 1.8. It may be that there is a life cycle process for the first decade of a marriage in which high satisfactions decline and then rebound as husband and wife work out their adjustment to one another. It also is theoretically possible that there are cohort differences and that those who have been married nine and ten years were always happier than those who have been married seven or eights years. In the latter case, if we should look at the same respondents five years from now, those who have been married five or six years now, and will be married ten or eleven years then, will still be lower than those who are older than them and those who are younger in marriage satisfaction.

There is no absolute way on the basis of the present data to choose between the cohort effect and life cycle, although the apparently parallel religious "U-curve" described in the preliminary Knights of Columbus report was established to be a life cycle and not a cohort phenomenon. It seems reasonable and probable that we are dealing (Table 1.8) with a life cycle effect, and this report will assume the life cycle explanation as the more probable of the two. The question can be finally settled only when the same couples are followed through the phases of their marriage. In the absence of "longitudinal" analysis in which individuals or populations are followed through phases, one must be content with the cross sectional analysis to be attempted in this report -- analysis which assumes that different levels of satisfaction at different ages represent a process of life cycle decline and growth.

The decline and growth phenomenon is much sharper for women than for men (Table 1.9). In fact, the level of marital satisfaction for men does not decline at all in the first decade of marriage and increases somewhat in the final two years of the decade. Satisfaction for women begins in the early years of a marriage to be higher than that for men, but after the second year declines sharply from 82 percent to 55 percent and then even more sharply in the seventh and eighth year to 46 percent. Thus, in the first eight years of marriage while men's marital satisfaction does not change, women's declines almost by half. However, in the last two years of the cycle women's marital satisfaction sharply rebounds and reaches a high level comparable with that of men. It would appear, then, (though our case base is very thin) that somewhere between the eighth and the tenth year of marriage problems in the relationship are worked out which leads to an enormous increase in the marital satisfaction of the wife.

The life cycle in the first decade of marriage is also notable in matters of "sexual fulfillment", "emotional satisfaction", and "value consensus". In each there is a sharp decline in the middle years of marriage and for sexual fulfillment and value consensus, a rebound in the last few years of the decade (on all three of these variables, there is very little difference between men and women in the process of decline and growth).

There are then three problems to be analyzed in greater detail: the impact of children on sexual fulfillment and the reason for both the lower level of emotional satisfaction among women, the sharper decline of that satisfaction, and then in the last two years of the decade its extraordinary resurgence. Finally, we will want to investigate the phenomenon of the lower level of marital satisfaction of religiously mixed marriages.

It is not having children but having one child (the first one, obviously) which leads to a decline in sexual and emotional quality of the marriage relationship (Table 1.11). There are practically no differences between those who have no children and those who have two or more children in either of these measures. (Nor are there are differences between men and women on either of these measures by number of children.) Whether it is the trauma to the relationship of having a new member in the family, or a trauma caused by the duration of marriage -- into the troubled middle years of the first decade -- a time which happens to coincide with the coming of the first child is an interesting issue for which at least a partial answer may be provided by Table 1.12. The decline in sexual fulfillment between the first two years and the second two years of marriage occurs whether one has no child or one child. Thus it is the duration of the marriage, not the presence of the child, which seems to be responsible for the initial decline. However, by the fifth and sixth year of marriage, the sexual fulfillment has gone up again for those who have no children and plunged to a very low 12 percent for those who have one child. While at the same time, those who have two or more children are indistinguishable from those who have no children in their level of sexual fulfillment (53 percent for the former and 52 percent for the latter). Thus, a combination of troubled middle years of the decade and the presence of one child leads to an enormous deterioration of the sexual fulfillment for those who have only one child. However, those who have no children or who have two or more children have already begun to experience by the sixth year a rebound in sexual fulfillment. It is only in the ninth and the tenth year of the marriage that those who have one child achieve parity in sexual fulfillment with those who have no children or who have two or more children. To summarize the findings by way of artificial advice: those troubled at the prospect of a decline in sexual fulfillment in the middle years of the first decade of a marriage should either have no children at all or rather quickly have a second child.

Obviously, there are some very interesting questions about the dynamics of the marriage relationship in the middle years of the first decade and the subtle and intricate impact on that relationship; the problems and frictions which arise with the passage of time, and the impact of the first child. Both factors seem to be at work at least somewhat independently of each other, though by the end of the first decade the sexual fulfillment has rebounded no matter how many children a respondent has. It may very well rebound earlier for those who have two children; not because having a second child improves the sexual relationship, but because the improvement of sexual relationship is a motivation for having a second child. However, these intricate issues cannot be analyzed by our present modestly sized sample.

There is no correlation between a wife's marital satisfaction and her own rating of the sexual fulfillment of their relationship. Thus, one cannot say on the basis of the wife's testimony that sexual problems are responsible for the sharp decline in her marriage satisfaction in the middle years of the decade and that the resolution of the problem of sexual fulfillment is responsible for the rise in her marital satisfaction.

However, we have, in addition to the wife's evaluation of the "excellence" of the sexual fulfillment of the marriage, also the husband's evaluation and it turns out that when a husband evaluates the sexual fulfillment of the marriage as excellent, there is no difference between the wives' marital satisfaction and the marital satisfaction of men (Table 1.13). Approximately three-quarters of the men and of the women with men who say that their sexual fulfullment is 'excellent' are 'very satisfied' with the marriage, while only one-half of the women whose husbands are less enthusiastic in endorsing the 'excellence' of the sexual relationship report themselves 'very satisfied".

The matter is intricate to describe and perhaps difficult to understand. From a woman's questionnaire we know both her marital satisfaction and her estimate of the sexual fulfillment of the relationship. There is no correlation between those two items. But we also have another view of the relationship -- that of her husband -- and if _he_ thinks the sexual fulfillment is not "excellent" then _her_ evaluation of the satisfaction of the marriage is likely to be much lower. A response, in other words, on the husband's questionnaire predicts the marital satisfaction of the wife much better than does the response on her own questionnaire.

There are a number of possible explanations for this phenomenon. A woman may perceive that there is something wrong with the marriage and hence tend to give it a lower satisfaction ranking, but not perceive that the problem is a matter of sexual fulfillment. Or she may understand that the problem is sexual

fulfillment but be reluctant to say it or at least to report it on a survey

questionnaire. Or it may finally be that the husband perceives the problem as

sexual, but has not been able to communicate this to his wife. Or it may be

a combination of these three explanations or other explanations -- none of which

are able to be tested against the present modestly sized data set.

Furthermore, the husband's perception of the sexual fulfillment of the

marriage declines very sharply in the middle years of the first decade (Table 1.14);

from 45 percent saying that it is excellent at the beginning of the marriage, to

only one-third saying that it is excellent in the mid-years of the decade, and only

one-fifth saying that it is excellent in the seventh and eighth year of the

marriage. However, in the last two years there is a sharp rebound back to the

original level for 46 percent of the men reporting excellent sexual fulfillment

in their marriage. Something then dramatic seems to happen between many husbands

and wives between the eighth and tenth year of their marriage which leads to a

dramatic improvement in the husband's perception in the quality of their sex

life.

It also would appear (Table 1.15) that this ebb and flow of the husband's

sexual fulfillment in the marriage explains a good deal of the decline and then

rebirth of the wife's description of her marriage satisfaction. Those whose

husbands say the sexual fulfillment is excellent never fall lower than 65 percent

being "very satisfied" with their marriage, while their counterparts whose

husbands are not so pleased with sexual fulfillment decline to 48 percent in

marital satisfaction. The former group rebounds between the eighth and tenth

year to 90 percent while the latter rebounds to 60 percent saying they are "very

satisfied" with their marriage.

Thus, we can summarize by observing that the lower proportion of women saying they are "very satisfied" with their marriage is almost entirely a phenomenon of sexual adjustment -- as the sexual adjustment is reported by the husband; in great part (although, of course, not entirely) the dramatic decline and then the sharp improvement in the level of marital satisfaction of women can be attributable to the decline and then the rise in the feeling of sexual fulfillment by their husbands. Finally, there is clearly a critical turning point in the young Catholic family between the eighth and tenth year of marriage in which both marital satisfaction and sexual adjustment which had declined sharply from the early years now rises again dramatically. In a subsequent chapter we will try to ascertain whether religion has any impact on this decline and growth.

Religiously mixed marriages (Table 1.16) begin at virtually the same level of satisfaction as do Catholic marriages. But the decline in the satisfaction level of mixed marriages is much sharper, falling to a low of 55 percent reporting that they are "very satisfied" in the middle years of the first decade, as opposed to 71 percent "very satisfied" at the same time among Catholic marriages. The "rebound" effect is much sharper in the Catholic marriage -- rising to 89 percent saying they are "very satisfied" at the end of the decade as opposed to 65 percent of those in mixed marriages. Thus, always acknowledging the weaknesses of our limited sample size, we are able to say that across time a mixed marriage declines more sharply and rebounds more slowly than does a marriage between two Catholics.

Finally, "living together" seems to be a much less satisfactory relationship than marriage -- despite the folk wisdom among young people to the contrary. Only half of those who are living together say their relationship is "very satisfied" as opposed to two-thirds of those who are married. As might be expected, there is

also a statistically significant relationship between living together and low
satisfaction with the "stability" of the relationship. Forty-nine percent of
those who are married described the stability of their relationship as "excellent"
as opposed to 20 percent of those who are living together.

It is precisely (Table 1.19) this instability which is responsible for the
lower levels of satisfaction among those who are living together. There are no
statistically significant differences between the two groups when perception of
stability is taken into account. If you don't think your relationship is
"excellent" in stability, then being married doesn't add significantly to your
satisfaction with the relationship. From the point of view of satisfaction,
you might as well be living together without marriage.

One might assume that the instability of living together would be more of
a burden to a young woman who might be expected, on the basis of tradition, to
be more concerned about the stability of a relationship, and that men could
survive the instability of living together with much less impediment to their
satisfaction with the relationship. However (Table 1.20), if the playboy
philosophy applies to anyone in our sample of young Catholics, it applies to
the women in "living together" relationships. There is no difference in the
proportion of "very satisfied" among women who are married and women who are
living together, but a statistically significant difference for men -- 74 percent
of the men who are married say they are "very satisfied" with the relationship
as opposed to 33 percent of those who are living together. Thus, young Catholic men
seem to find the fashion of living together without marriage and the resultant
instability a much greater burden than do young Catholic women. The limited number
of cases makes it impossible for us to press this unexpected finding by any
further analysis.

SUMMARY

1) A history of divorce affects negatively the satisfaction of a present marriage.

2) Mixed marriages are less satisfying, especially with the passage of time, since they rebound less dramatically from the crisis of the middle years of the first decade.

3) Similarly, invalid marriages are less likely to be satisfying than marriages at which a priest has officiated.

4) Living together because of its instability is less likely to be a satisfying relationship, especially for men.

5) The marriages of Catholics who are not white are much less likely to be satisfying, presumably because of poverty.

6) Many marriages go through deterioration in the middle of the first decade and then rebound towards the end of the decade. Satisfaction in a marriage, both general and specificially sexual, takes a long time to build.

7) Children do not seem to impede the general satisfaction level of marriages, nor do they impede the sexual fulfillment save for those couples who have only one child during the middle years of the first decade of their marriage. For this group, sexual fulfillment seems virtually to collapse.

8) The average satisfaction level for women seems to be a result of the sexual fulfillment aspect of the marriage, particularly as perceived by their husbands. The decline in sexual fulfillment parallels a sharp decline in marital satisfaction for women and the resurgence of marital satisfaction in the last two years of the first decade for women is caused in part by a notable improvement in sexual fulfillment (as perceived by their husbands) of their marriage.

9) Thus, there is no confirmation of the pietistic position taken by some Catholics that sexual fulfillment is not important to marriage satisfaction.

10) The improvement of both sexual fulfillment and marriage satisfaction (as well as value consensus) between the eighth and the tenth year of marriage represents the decisive and critical turning point in the history of a marriage relationship in which many husbands and wives seem to be able to dramatically resolve some of the problems that effect their relationship and notably improve the quality of their married life.

Chapter Two - Joint Marital Happiness

The first chapter of this report dealt for the most part with individual respondents. Spouses' responses were invoked only to explain the lower propensity of young Catholic women to say that their marriages were "very satisfying". In this chapter, we turn to the discussion not of individual ratings of "satisfaction" and "excellence" of the marriage, but to a study of the marriage relationship itself as described by both spouses. A relationship is considered henceforth in this report to be "very satisfying" only if both spouses describe it as such and a "relationship rating" is considered to be "excellent" only if both spouses assert that it is "excellent". To the extent that such descriptions and ratings are an accurate reflection of the quality of marriage life, one could say with some measure of confidence that we are dealing with reasonably happy marriages.

By this standard, about one-half of the Catholics in the United States (56 percent) are in marriages in which both partners say the relationship is "very satisfactory". The "mini life cycle" is almost perfectly reflected in Table 2.1. Sixty-five percent of the couples are "very satisfied" in the first two years of marriage. The proportion declines to fifty percent from the third to the eighth year*, and seventy percent -- higher even than in the first two years -- in the last two years of the first decade of marriage. Obviously something extremely important happens between the eighth and tenth year of a Catholic marriage.

Is this decline and resurgence of marital satisfaction a function of actual duration of the marriage or is it part of an age cycle which happens to coincide with the marriage cycle? If we compare those marriages in which the primary respondent is between 25 and 27 and those in which the primary respondent is between 28 and 30, we see that the marriage cycle seems to be a phenomenon of

---

*We combine the middle years into one "3-8" category to faciliate tests for statistical significance.

the duration of marriage itself and not to be a function of the age of respondents. (Thus, our assumption that we are dealing with a life cycle rather than a cohort effect gains some support.)

How much agreement is there between husband and wife on the quality of their marriage relationships? The ratings of marriage by husbands and wives strongly correlate (Table 2.2) but there is by no means unanimity. Indeed, one can explain at the most one-quarter of the variance in one spouse's scale by the variance in the other spouse's scale (variance explanation is measured by squaring the correlation between two variables). There are, in other words, many married people who think their relationships are excellent but this rating of their relationship is not confirmed by their spouse.

The ability to talk to one another, emotional satisfaction, sexual fulfillment, the ability to communicate love and affection, the ability to express disagreement without threatening the relationship seem to be the most powerful predictors of a satisfying marriage relationship (Table 2.3). However, since these variables are strongly intercorrelated with one another, it is necessary to sort out the ones that really matter. A multiple regression equation revealed (Table 2.4) that sexual fulfillment, value consensus, and emotional satisfaction are the statistically significant predictors of a happy marital relationship.

Just as marriage satisfaction goes through a life cycle in the first decade of the marriage, so does sexual fulfillment, value consensus, and emotional satisfaction. Sexual fulfillment declines from 34 percent to 21 percent and then rebounds to 42 percent. Value consensus declines from 26 percent to 16 percent and rebounds to 33 percent. Emotional satisfaction varies from 22 percent to 13 percent, back to 20 percent.

The impact of this variation in marriage ratings on marital satisfaction through the first decade of the marriage is strikingly illustrated in Tables 2.6 and 2.7. The overwhelming majority of those who say that their sexual fulfillment is excellent are "very satisfied" with the general quality of their marriage through the whole of the life cycle; though there is, even among this group, a decline (from 86 percent to 78 percent) in the middle years of the marriage.

On the other hand, those whose sexual fulfillment is not excellent begin at a lower level of satisfaction (58 percent in the first two years of marriage), decline to a much lower level (45 percent), and rebound much less sharply (up five percentage points in the final two years of the decade).

Virtually the same pattern exists in the relationship among joint satisfaction with the marriage, joint rating of values as "excellent", and the duration of the marriage. Both groups have a decline in the middle years but those who agree on values are at all times higher in their marital satisfaction than those who disagree (just as those who have a jointly described "excellent" sexual relationship even in their worst years are more satisfied with the marriage than those who do not have a good sexual fulfillment are satisfied in their best years).

Thus, sexual fulfillment and value consensus are enormously important both to the quality of the marriage relationship and to the durability of a high quality in the relationship and the working out of values problems and sexual problems seems to be decisively important to improving the quality of marriage. One can say with some confidence that the change in a marriage between the eighth and the tenth year in substantial part must be attributable to an improvement in value consensus and sexuality in the relationship between the husband and the wife. To anticipate one of the conclusions of this report, if the church is interested in ministry to people who are in the critical turning point of the late years of the first decade of the marriage, it must be prepared both to facilitate the emergence of a value consensus and to facilitate the improvement of the quality of their sexual life. There is little question that the church has the interest and the ability to tend to the values issue. It is much less clear that it can cope with sexual problems.

Both the ability to express love and affection (as perceived by the two spouses) and the ability to express disagreement without threatening the relationship goes through the now familiar first decade life cycle. Spouses are equally satisfied at the beginning and at the end of the first decade of their marriage with their ability to express love for one another (27 percent in both cases). But the proportion saying that they can adequately express love and affection falls to half of that during the middle years of the decade. Similarly, their ability to work out conflict also falls almost by half in the course of a decade of marriage. In the eighth and the tenth year of marriage, in other words, many couples acquire an ability to express love and affection, as well as conflict, which they thought they had in the early years and then lost in the middle years (Table 2.7).

It should be noted, incidentally, that we are speaking of a population group and not of individuals. While the level of ability to deal with love and/or conflict in the general population declines, there are individuals who continue to maintain presumably their abilities to deal with these problems. Our research does not enable us to measure the ebb and the flow of the intensity of an individual couple's skills, rather it measures the intensity of such skills in the general Catholic population.

Contrary to the conventional wisdom, there is no relationship whatsoever between a respondent's attitude on certain questions of sexual
morality and either the quality of his marriage relationship as perceived by
the respondent and the spouse or their joint satisfaction with the excellence
of their sexual fulfillment (Table 2.8). Traditional teachings on divorce,
birth control, premarital sex, and living together do not relate either to a
satisfying marriage or a sexually fulfilling one. On the other hand, more
liberal attitudes on these issues do not promote either a more satisfying or
sexually fulfilling relationship. Sexual values -- in so far as they can be
measured by attitudes on divorce, birth control, premarital sex, and living
together -- seem to have nothing to do with the quality of a relationship
that develops between a man and woman once they are married (it ought to be
noted that we are here speaking of attitudes, not of premarital behavior, since
we know nothing of the premarital behavior of the respondents in this project).

It will be recalled that there were moderately high correlations between
marriages rated jointly as excellent in their expressions of love and of disagreement and satisfaction with the marriage. However, neither of these variables
turned out to have a statistically significant direct relationship with joint
marital satisfaction. A series of informal colloquia that have occurred in
recent years between American sociologists and theologians (as a result of the
disastrous "Vatican Council III" meeting of the international journal Concilium
at Notre Dame in 1977) suggested that the capacity to work out both positive
feelings of love and negative feelings of anger in a sexual relationship would
contribute considerably to marital satisfaction. The graphs presented in
Tables 2.9 and 2.10 show that this expectation has been confirmed. "Disagreement"
and "love" have their impact on this satisfaction with the quality of a marriage
relationship, indirectly through their impact, both on sexual fulfillment, and

on values. It is worth noting that while the ability to express disagreement without threatening a marriage relates equally to sexual fulfillment and values, that love has a far more powerful indirect impact on joint satisfaction through sexual fulfillment than it does through value consensus. A couple's capacity to disagree and to love as these capacities are reflected in their sexual life plays a considerable part in shaping their marital satisfaction.

So we again anticipate pastoral conclusion. Love, values, anger and sex, often related to one another, are quite important in facilitating the quality of married life. Love and disagreement have their impact not so much directly, but through their effect on values and especially on sexuality. The church, which purports to minister to people in the crises of their married life, must be especially able to deal with the problems of love, sex and conflict.

Summary

1. About half of the young Catholic marriages were rated as "very satisfactory" by both partners. After a crisis for many marriages in the middle years of the first decade, some seven out of ten young Catholic families are described as "very satisfactory" by both husband and wife.

2. Sexual fulfillment, value consensus and emotional satisfaction are the most powerful predictors of joint satisfaction with the marriage. Values and emotional satisfaction to some extent, and sexual fulfillment to a very considerable extent, go through a parallel life cycle decline and rise.

3. The proportion of young Catholic marriages which are jointly described as "excellent" in their sexual fulfillment doubles from the middle years to the last years in the first decade of marriage.

4. Sexual fulfillment in marriage is an exremely powerful predictor of whether a marriage goes into a decline in the middle years of the first decade and how deep that decline is.

5. There is no relationship at all between "liberal" attitudes on birth control, premarital sex, and living together, on the one hand, and marital satisfaction excellence and sexual fulfillment on the other. Neither is there any relationship between conservative attitudes on these issues and marital happiness.

6. The capacity to express love and to express disagreement does not relate directly to joint satisfaction with the quality of a marriage, but indirectly to their impact on value consensus and especially on sexual fulfillment.

7. Love, conflict, values and sex seem to be the components of the dramatic crisis -- normally a crisis of growth -- which affects young Catholic marriages during the final years of their first decade.

Chapter Three - Religion & Marital Happiness

We have observed in previous chapters that to some considerable extent marital satisfaction is shaped directly by emotional contentment, value consensus, sexual fulfillment in marriage, and indirectly by the capacity of the spouses to express both love and conflict in the marriage relationship, especially when love and conflict impinge on their sexual fulfillment. We now turn to the question of whether religious devotion has any effect on marital adjustment. It seems safe to assume that many of those scholars, Christian and non-Christian, who are convinced that the world has become "secularized" and that religion has little impact on daily human life, would not expect religious devotion to notably influence marital satisfaction and especially not to influence sexual fulfillment. However, Table 3.1 indicates that when husbands and wives both pray frequently (not necessarily together), when they both go to church frequently (again, not necessarily together), and when they both believe in the after life, these forms of religious devotion are likely to have a statistically significant impact on their marriage relationship. Indeed, of the nine correlations in Table 3.1, the only one to be statistically insignificant is the one which one might most likely expect to be significant -- the relationship between frequent church attendance and value consensus. Particularly it is worth noting that all three kinds of devotion affect the consensus between husband and wife that their sexual fulfillment is "excellent".

The correlations, while significant, are modest as they will be in most tables for the remainder of this report. In matters as nebulous and as undefined (necessarily so given the limitations of the secondary analysis being attempted in this presentation) as marital happiness the investigator does not expect huge correlations. Statistically significant correlations in the directions hypothesized either by instinct or, as in the subsequent chapter, by theory is all that the researcher could ask for. Such correlations should be sufficient (hopefully) to indicate to the administrator, the pastoral worker, and the theologian, the dynamics of human intimate relationships on which they ought to reflect.

There are also statistically significant correlations between such matters as mixed marriage, a valid marriage, and a marriage after divorce, and various forms of marital contentment. Thus, whether a couple was married by a priest influences both their general satisfaction and their joint rating of their sexual relationship as "excellent" (perhaps it ought to be noted here that a "joint" rating as "excellent" means that both spouses on their separate questionnaires have rated the marriage as "excellent", not that they have worked together to achieve this description of their relationship). The religiously mixed marriage has a negative effect on value consensus, and marriage after a divorce has a negative effect on whether both husband and wife consider their marriage to be "very satisfactory".

Religion then does have some influence on the quality of Catholic marriage. If both spouses pray frequently, if they both go to church frequently, if they believe in life after death, and if they were married by a priest, they are somewhat more likely to describe their marriage as very satisfactory and their sexual fulfillment as excellent. Frequent prayer and belief in life after death also affect their joint rating of their value consensus. Mixed marriages negatively influence value consensus. Divorce negatively influences general marital happiness.

These correlations are illustrated in percentages in Tables 3.2 to 3.5.
Sixty-four percent of those families in which both spouses go to church say
that their marriage is "very satisfactory" as opposed to 51 percent in which
either or both do not go to church. Similarly, 37 percent of the church-goers
say their sexual fulfillment is "excellent" as opposed to 25 percent of the
others, and 29 percent say their value consensus is "excellent" as opposed
to 19 percent of the others. Virtually the same percentage distributions
apply when one considers the influence of frequent prayer and belief in
life after death, and of the nine relationships inspected in Tables 3.2, 3.3,
and 3.4, eight are statistically significant. Those who go to church more
often, pray more often, and believe in life after death, have more satisfactory
and more sexually fulfilling, more value consensual marriages. Presumably,
it is religion that affects marital happiness and not vice versa. One can
imagine, for example, that the hopefulness that comes with belief in life after
death would account for believers being half again as likely to say jointly
that their sexual fulfillment is "excellent", rather than the sexual fulfillment
making them more likely to believe in life after death. Nonetheless, in the real
world there is probably a reciprocal causality, with belief in life after death
generating the hopefulness which is necessary for the risk taking of sexual
intimacy and the satisfactions of such intimacy strengthening the conviction
of husband and wife that they live in a universe that is more benign than not.
To piece out the intricate dynamics of such a reciprocal flow of influence is
beyond the capabilities available to us from the present data set and indeed
from any investigation but elaborate longitudinal research.

Marriage by a priest and the absence of a previous marriage (Table 3.5)
both relate statistically to satisfaction in marriage. If they were married

by a priest, 58 percent of both the spouses say their marriage is "very

satisfactory" as opposed to 49 percent of those who were not married by

a priest. Fifty-seven percent of those who were not divorced say their

marriage is "very satisfactory" as opposed to 41 percent of those cases in

which one or the other spouse has been divorced.

In a previous chapter we noted that an individual respondent's description

of whether his marriage was "very satisfactory" was affected by whether the

marriage was "Catholic" or "mixed". The deterioration of satisfaction in mixed

marriages was sharper; the rebound from the deterioration less vigorous than was

true in Catholic marriages. Table 3.6 confirms the same basic picture when one

looks not at the individual view of marriage but the joint view. At the

beginning of a decade of married life, there is no difference in the satisfaction

levels of both Catholic and mixed marriages. However, at the end of the decade,

after a sharp decline in mixed marriages and a somewhat less sharp decline for

Catholic marriages, the Catholic marriage is 5 percentage points higher in

the proportion saying that they are "very satisfied" than was true at the

beginning of the marriage; whereas in the mixed marriage, the proportion in

which both spouses say they are "very satisfied" is 6 points lower. The two

marriages begin at the same level of satisfaction but the Catholic marriage,

at the end of a decade, is 11 percentage points more likely to be described as

"very satisfactory" by both respondents.

Both joint commitment to the Catholic Church and joint commitment to

certain religious practices affect the first decade of the marriage life cycle

(Table 3.6B), especially towards the end of the life cycle. In the

middle of the marriage, both those who are high on the religion scale (made up

of a combination of joint church attendance, joint belief in life after death, and joint prayer) are at an all time low with a portion saying that they are both "very satisfied" with the marriage. Both rebound in the final years of the decade, but the religious marriage from 62 percent "very satisfied" to 82 percent, and the less religious marriage from 44 percent to 58 percent. The couple, in other words, in which both spouses are devout, seems to have a much better chance to work its way through the crisis point between the eighth and the tenth year of marriage. The "rebound" for the religious marriages is "statistically significant"; for the other marriages it is not.

They also have a much better chance of working through their problems of sexual fulfillment and value consensus (Table 3.8). Both devout and less devout rebound from that crisis, but the devout seem to do so much more dramatically whether it be in general marital satisfaction, sexual fulfillment, or value consensus. Shared religious commitment, then, seems to especially facilitate shared satisfaction and shared fulfillment at the turning point in the latter years of the first decade of marriage (and satisfaction and fulfillment may also in turn lead to great religious devotion). However, as we noted before, married couples see no change in the explicit religious consensus in their lives. It may well be the case that they are unaware of the relationship among religion, sexuality, value, and satisfaction that intensifies the second half of the first decade of their marriage. The rebound for those high on sexual fulfillment or value consensus is statistically significant; for their opposite numbers the rebound is not "significant".

The model in Table 3.9 describes one possible causal flow in the relationship of religious devotion, marital quality, and marital satisfaction (as all these variables are measured by agreement between husband and wife, either in behavior, as in the case of religious devotion, or in description as "excellent" in the

case of value and fulfillment, or in description as "very satisfied" as in the
case of marital satisfaction by both). Religious devotion has a direct influence
on marital satisfaction and also an indirect influence through its impact on
sexual fulfillment and value consensus. The more devout a couple is, the more
likely they are to think of their marriage as sexually fulfilling and as
enjoying value consensus and these new characteristics, as well as religious
devotion, directly also lead to a greater propensity of the couple to describe
their marriage as "very satisfactory". The more religious a Catholic marriage
is, both in devotion and in its sacramental origin, the more mutally fulfilling
a marriage is likely to be and the more satisfying to both husband and wife.
These relationships grow stronger rather than weaker with the passage of time.

Summary

1. Both the belief in life after death and church attendance -- when both
   spouses are involved in these attitudes and behavior -- lead to
   higher levels of marital fulfillment. The more religious a couple is,
   the happier they are in their marriage.

2. A sacramental marriage between two Catholics is also more satisfying
   and more fulfilling sexually than a mixed marriage. This satisfaction
   becomes especially pronounced towards the end of the first decade of
   the marriage, as the sacramental marriage rebounds more vigorously
   from the crisis of the middle years of the first decade of marriage.

3. Religious devotion also facilitates the rebound of a marriage towards
   the end of the first decade both in terms of general satisfaction of
   both spouses with the relationship and also in their agreement that
   their sexuality and their value consensus are "excellent." The family
   that prays together may not stay together longer, but the family in

which both husband and wife pray seems to improve the quality of the relationship the longer it stays together.

4. Religious devotion influences marital satisfaction both directly and indirectly, the latter through its influence on sexual fulfillment and value consensus.

Chapter Four - Religious Images, Religious Experience, and Marital Happiness

It is appropriate to begin this chapter with a brief summary of the theory of the sociology of religion which has directed the present analysis and in particular a segment of it will be presented in this chapter. A more detailed elaboration of the theory can be found in William McCready and Andrew Greeley, Ultimate Values of the American Population, and Andrew Greeley, forthcoming, Religion: A Secular Theory.

Religion, it is assumed by this theory, is rooted in the human capacity to hope; a capacity which Lionel Tiger has recently suggested may be genetic, but is, in any case, uneradicable. Reinforcing this propensity to hope, and probably a consequent of it, is the human capacity to experience moments of "gratuity"; such moments (David Tracy in Blessed Rage for Order calls them limit experiences) may be relatively minor such as a beautiful summer day, a cold silent sheet of ice on the lake in winter time, a touch of a friendly hand, a smile of a two year old, or they may be the major ecstatic experiences of the sort described by William James, or any kind of intense moments of "revelation" or "gratuity", that would appear on a continuum between these extremes (for greater detail and discussion of these experiences, see Blessed Rage for Order, John Shea's Stories of God, and Andrew Greeley's The Mary Myth). These moments of gratuity -- they may also be called moments of 'grace" -- are "sacrements" (with a small s), or "revelations" (with a small r) which seem to reveal a secret design or purpose or goodness or order at work in this cosmos. In these expriences of "grace", one may find the origin both of religious heritages which developed through history and of the religious perspectives which developed through the biography of an individual person.

These experiences are resonated and recounted to a person as "symbols" or "images" or "pictures" which spontaneously arrise in his own imaginative process to help him to articulate what he has experienced. Such "symbols" are drawn both from his own religious tradition and from the general repertoire of powerful imagery which is at the disposal of humankind (sun, moon, light, water, fire, food, sex, etc., etc.). Often the core of religious heritage can be found by examining what use it makes of the human symbol repertoire.

Such religious symbols resonating, representing, and articulating -- still at the imaginative level and in the imaginative dimension of the personality -- are in fact "stories" which purport to provide meaning both to the life of the individual person and the existence of the cosmos. These religious stories implicitly and imaginatively link the experiences of an individual's life with that Higher Order which he has experienced in his moments of "gratuity" or "grace" (it is not relevant for the purposes of this report, but one might add that in this approach to religion Sacraments (with a capital S) and Revelations (with a capital R) are those experiences and symbols -- the death and resurrection of Jesus for example -- in which a given religious tradition emphatically reaffirms, confirms, validates, and revalidates the fundamental moments of hopefulness that all humans encounter in their lives.)

A religious symbol then is an articulation of an experience of hope. Such symbols are implicitly "stories" which link the stories of a life of an individual person with what the person perceives to be the Larger Story of the cosmos. Such symbols not only represent for the person and give meaning for what has happened so far in his own story, but they also shape the development of that story since they describe the "scenery" and the "setting" with which the rest of his story will unroll.

All of this activity occurs initially and primordially in the creative
or the imaginative dimension of the personality; that which is called
by Leonard Kube, "the preconscious and the creative imagination," by
Jacques Maritain, "the creative faculty," and "agent intellect" (here Maritain
would be following Aquinas and Aristotle) and by St. Paul, "our spirit"
(to which The Spirit speaks). Since humans are more than imaginative and poetic
creatures, they very quickly reflect intellectually on, philosophize about, and
then   theologize about their moments of grace and then express a digested
version of these theologies in credal statements and catechetical propositions.
Such statements and propositions, of course , are "religious" but they are
not primordially religious in the sense that the experiences of grace and
the stories which produce these experiences can be said to be primordially
and fundamentally religious. If one wishes to know then the religious orientation
of a human personality, one must look to his/her catechetical propositions and
credal statements but also and more importantly to his/her religious imagery and
the stories implicit in such imagery. For the purpose of the present research
we are assuming that the experiences of childhood relationships are "sacramental"
in that they reveal to a child something about the nature of the cosmos and the
possibility of his own existence. We assume that these experiences of childhood
affect an adult's religious imagery and that religious imagery in turn affects
his approach to human intimacy and human love. Quite simply put, the warmer
the childhood experiences have been, the warmer a person's religious imagery
will be; the warmer will be his own marital intimacy. No argument is made that
all the religious imagery is shaped by childhood experience or that all of the
quality of the warmth of the marriage is shaped by the warmth of religious
imagery that a husband and wife may have. Such an expectation would be absurd

because both religious imagery and marital satisfaction are complex

phenomena likely to be shaped by many different aspects of a person's biological,

psychological, cultural and biographic background. We do not, in other words,

expect particularly high correlations among the variables with which we will

be working but we do expect there to be real and statistically significant

correlations.

If the experiences of the family of origin are revelatory, so, too, are the

experiences of the family of procreation. Husbands and wives "reveal" to one

another whether the "Real" is benign or malign, "warm" or "cold". When two

people marry they merge their individual stories into a common story. "Your"

story and "my" story become "our" story. Your religious imagery influences

my religious imagery, and vice versa. Therefore, in the course of the marriage,

there will be a tendency for husband and wife to converge in their religious

imagery. Convergence will in part be the result of their experiences of love,

but will also have a profound influence on the further development of their

marital satisfaction. Husband and wife are a "sacrament" for one another,

"grace" for one another (in the sociological if not the theological sense).

Therefore, a substantial amount of the ebb and flow, the rise and decline, and

rise again of the quality of their relationship will be interpretable in terms

of the changing patterns of their religious imagery.

The propositions in the previous paragraph may seem reasonable enough when

one reads them. Unfortunately for the empirical sociologist, it is not enough

to articulate plausible and attractive ideas. One must submit such ideas to

falsification or verification against empirical data. One must, for example in

this report, test the possibility that those who are more likely to think of

God as a lover are also more likely to be better lovers themselves -- a proposition

which, as I remarked in the introduction, would seem ridiculous to the sophisticated

conventional wisdom.

In order to state the hypotheses tested in this chapter as explicitly as possible, they are schematized in the following eight paragraphs:

1) Family experiences in childhood will affect religious image of an adult and through that imagery marital happiness. The warmer the childhood, the "warmer" the religious imagery.

2) Warm religious imagery will in turn affect both the capacity to express love and the capacity for sexual fulfillment. The warmer the religious imagery of husband and wife (as expressed in a joint measure), the more likely they will both be to describe a "warm" (i.e. "excellent") situation in their family with regard to both sexual fulfillment and capacity for loving.

3) In turn marital satisfaction (both "very satisfied") will be to a considerable extent shaped by "warm" religious imagery and "warm" sexual fulfillment.

4) As a marriage develops, there will be stronger correlations between the wife's religious imagery and the husband's religious imagery.

5) Much of the decline in sexual fulfillment and its subsequent rise will be explainable by a model which takes into account family "warmth", religious "warmth", and the perceived capacity to love.

6) Much of the decline in marital satisfaction and its subsequent rise will be explainable by a model which takes into account family "warmth", religious "warmth", the perceived capacity to love, and sexual fulfillment.

7) Religious warmth and sexual fulfillment will be the critical
   variables in the rebound of marriages at the end of their
   first decade.

8) Those who have intense religious experiences will have warmer
   religious imagery and hence more satisfying marriages.

Figure 4.1 states in analytic form hypotheses 1 to 3 and 5 to 7. Figure
4.2 expresses schematically proposition number eight (it is a much less
elaborate pathchart because only a very small proportion of respondents
have frequent ecstatic experiences of the sort described by William James,
and hence, the very simple analysis of the impact of these experiences (as
opposed to the experiences of a happy childhood and a happy marriage which
are far more frequent).

The strongest images of Jesus (the one's most likely to attract an
"extremely likely" rating from our respondents) are "gentle," "warm,"
"patient" and "comforting." There is little difference between the United
States and Canada on these images, although the Canadians are somewhat more
likely to describe Jesus as distant (seventeen percent as opposed to eleven
percent). This difference is accounted for entirely by somewhat higher
"distant" score among French Canadians -- twenty percent.

The same images which are popular for Jesus are also popular for Mary --
indeed, even more popular with the mother of Jesus having an even "better"
public image than her son (I am indebted to my colleague, Teresa Sullivan,
for recalling to my mind the sentence of St. Bernard of Clarvaux: "If you
fear the father, go to the son; if you fear the son, go to the mother.").
Despite the apparant decline on Marion devotion among Catholics and lesser
emphasis on Mary in Catholic education her image among Catholic young people
continues to be quite impressive, although French Canadians are somewhat

less likely to think of her as warm (seven percent) than their English Canadian and American counterparts, and substantially more (thirty-four percent as opposed to nine percent for Americans) to think of her as distant.

The images of God show less affection. Seventy-four percent are extremely likely to think of Him as a creator, sixty-two percent as a father, fifty-seven percent as a protector, forty-four percent as a master, and forty-five percent as a redeemer. Only thirty percent of Americans are extremely likely to think of Him as a lover and twelve percent to think of Him as a mother (twenty-five percent of American young people think of God at least some of the time as a mother -- there is no appreciable difference between the sexes in this image as, indeed, there is in none of the images in Table 4.1). The French Canadians, however, are more than twice as likely than Americans to think of God as a lover (seventy percent) and also substantially more likely (twenty-one percent as opposed to twelve percent) to be "extremely likely" to think of God as a mother. There are, then, interesting cultural differences between the French Canadians and their North American counterpart in religious imagination. The French Canadians are more likely to think of Jesus and Mary as distant, less likely to think of Mary as warm and more likely to think of God as a lover and mother. Nonetheless, Mary has a warmer image among the French Canadians as among other North Americans.

There is a place of union first with God (sixty-four percent) and then with loved ones (fifty-six percent). The next most frequent "very likely" picture of heaven is as a place of peace and tranquility (about half of the respondents so describe it). A little more than a third of the respondents think of heaven as a"spiritual life involving our minds but not our bodies" and a place of"loving, intellectual communion" -- which may not be all that attractive to embodied creatures and which in the first case may also be false to Catholic doctrine. Interestingly enough, only four percent of the respondents are very likely to think of heaven as a "life of intense action," which it surely is if Catholic eschatology is taken seriously, and only a fifth of the respondents are very likely to think of it as a paradise of pleasure and delight, which also is orthodox Catholic teaching.

Four items were selected as measures of "warm" religious imagery -- God as a lover, Jesus as warm, Mary as warm, and the after life as a "paradise of pleasure and delight." (Each of these images, incidentally, is a story because it implies an ongoing relationship.)

A five point scale was constructed from these items for measuring the relationship between individual (as opposed to joint husband-wife) religious imagery and marital adjustment. The relationship as Table 4.1B demonstrates is quite powerful. Thirty-three percent of those who thought of none of the warm images as "extremely likely" reported excellent sexual fulfillment in marriage, as opposed to sixty-nine percent of those who checked all four as "extremely likely." Similarly, twenty-seven percent of those low on the scale described the value consensus in ther marriage as excellent, as opposed to sixty-three percent of those who were high on the scale. Religious images, then, do, indeed, affect the quality of married life as that quality is perceived by an individual respondent. But our concern in this chapter is, rather, the combined imagery of husband and wife, and how that affects their combined view of their marital satisfaction.

Some Catholic marriages are characterized by common religious imagery between husband and wife. In half of all of the marriages husband and wife both describe Jesus as warm and Mary as warm, but only twelve percent of them share an image of God as a lover and only five percent an image of the after life as a paradise of pleasure and delight (Table 4.2). On the other hand, if a married person thinks of God as a lover, or of heaven as a paradise, there is more likely to be a similar image in the mind of his/her spouse than there is likely to be a correlation between husbands' and wives' images of Jesus as warm and Mary as warm. In other words, if you think of Jesus as warm, there is not much reason to believe that your spouse has the same thought, but if you think of God as a lover or of heaven as a paradise of pleasure, there is a much higher probability (though still the correlations in Table 4.3 are rather low) that your spouse will have the same religious imagery.

Through factor analysis of religious image patterns and the spouses' religious image patterns a "joint religious image scale" was created. This scale (4.4) correlates positively and significantly with marital satisfaction, sexual fulfillment and value consensus. If there is an atmosphere in the marriage in which husband and wife tend to share warm religious imagery, then their marriage satisfaction, their sexual fulfillment and their value consensus are likely to be higher than if they do not share such religious imagery. How you imagine Jesus, God, Mary and the after life does, indeed, affect your marital satisfaction and your sexual fulfillment. Religious images do, indeed, have an impact on what goes on in the bedroom (though, of course, people need not be aware of this impact).

Table 4.5 presents these same findings as percentages. If husband and wife are on the high end of the religious warmth scale, they are 16 percentage points more likely to say that they are both very satisfied with the marriage, 14 percentage points more likely to both say that their sexual adjustment is excellent and 12 percentage points more likely to say that their value consensus is excellent. All three differences are statistically significant.

Religious warmth, in other words, is good for a marriage. Religious warmth and marital warmth correlate with one another.

Religious warmth declines in the middle years of the first decade of marriage, at the time spouses are experiencing an increase in problems in their marriage life and individual respondents are experiencing problems in their religious belief systems. However, in the last two years of the marriage the warmth scale seems to rebound to where it was at the beginning of the marriage. (Table 4.6).

Furthermore, as hypothesized in proposition four at the beginning of this chapter, there is much greater convergence between husband and wife in their religious imagery as the story of their marriage develops. In the last two years of the first decade of marriage there are strong and statistically significant correlations between husbands and wives in their view of God as a lover (.40) and their view of after life as a paradise of pleasure and delight (.23). Common religious imagery, then, does, indeed, tend to emerge out of the "story" of a common life together (Table 4.7).

The story of this convergence is dramatically illustrated in Table 4.8. In the first two years of marriage there is a very high probability that if your spouse says that God is a lover, you will think so. This proportion declines precipitously from 79 percent to 51 percent by the middle of the marriage. In other words, at that time your spouse's influence on your own image of God as a lover has practically fallen by .318. But then, in the final two years of the first decade of marriage the convergence becomes quite dramatic. Your spouse's image of God has a far more powerful impact on you than it has had since the first years of the marriage. On the other hand, if your spouse is not likely to think of God as a lover

(one must remember that respondent's imagery and spouse's imagery are

collected from different questionnaires), the deterioration of your own

image of God as a lover continues even into the ninth and the tenth year

of the marriage. The greatest difference between those whose spouse says

it is extremely likely that God is a lover and those whose spouse does not

say it is in the final two years of the decade. Sixty-seven percent of

those whose spouse says it is "extremely likely" that God is a lover,

themselves say that it is "extremely likely;" whereas only 12 percent of

those whose spouse says that it is not likely for them to think of God

as a lover, themselves say it is likely for them to think of God as a lover.

In other words, by the end of the first decade of marriage if your spouse

thinks of God as a lover, it is highly probable that you will. If your

spouse does not think that way, it is very unprobable that you will think

of God as a lover.

Furthermore, sexual fulfillment in marriage has a considerable impact

on the image of God as a lover. Seventy-one percent of those who say that

their sex life together is excellent say that God is a lover and their

spouse says that God is a lover. Only 56 percent of those with less than

excellent sexual adjustment reflect the spouse's conviction that God is

a lover. Precisely then, in those marriages where the sexual fulfillment

is high, there is the strongest relationship between a spouse's image of

God as a lover and one's own image of God as a lover. (Table 4. 8 B).

A small proportion of the population also think of God as a mother

(Table 4.9). Nineteen percent of our respondents are either extremely likely or somewhat likely to say that they imagine God as a mother. There is a statistically significant difference between those whose spouses have such an image and those whose spouses do not. Twenty-eight percent of those who have spouses who think of God as a mother share this imagination, whereas only seventeen percent of those whose spouses do not think of God as a mother have this imagination themselves. (Table 4.10).

The convergence of imagery of God as mother increases as the years of marriage increase (Table 4.11). While there are only enough cases in three of the cohorts to generate a coefficience of association (the so-called "gamma" statistic), the size of the coefficient between spouse's image of God as mother and respondent's image doubles between the third and the eighth year of marriage. Finally, (Table 4.12), the association between spouses on the subject of the maternity of God is much stronger in marriages in which the spouses are very satisfied (gamma = .37) than it is in marriages where both spouses are not very satisfied (gamma = .16). Thus, both marital satisfaction and the passage of time leads to a convergence, even of the somewhat unusual image of the maternity of God.

"Warm" religious imagery raises the marital satisfaction and sexual fulfillment, and husband-wife imagery converges after the mid-decade marital crisis, as a common marriage "story" evolves and a common repertoire of religious imagery tends to appear to resonate with the story, both influencing it and being influenced by it.

We have established, then, that religious imagery affects both sexual fulfillment and marital satisfaction. We now must turn to the question of whether family background experiences -- a warm family life and childhood -- also relate to present marital warmth. If such relationships exist, we then can put numbers on the paths presented in Figure 4.1 and formally test hypotheses one to three and five to seven as described earlier in this chapter.

There are statistically significant, though moderate, relationships between a respondent's description of happiness as a child and joint satisfaction with a marriage and joint sexual fulfillment in a marriage and value consensus in a marriage. There are also statistically significant relationships between closeness to the mother and joint satisfaction and value consensus, and between closeness to the father and sexual fulfillment. Happy and intimate childhoods, in other words, relate positively though modestly with happy marriages. (Table 4.13)

Furthermore, and finally, (Figure 4.3) adult religious imagery is related modestly but significantly to childhood experiences both of the respondent and the respondent's spouse. Warm religious imagery acts as a "funnel" which gathers together childhood influences and passes them on to marital evaluation. The joint religious imagery scale correlates significantly (at a level in excess of .2) both with "excellent" sexual fulfillment as reported by both spouses and "excellent" capacity to express love and affection as reported by both spouses. The love and affection capacity as we noted in a previous chapter does not directly relate to marital satisfaction but influences marital satisfaction through its connection with sexual fulfillment. To wrap up the package: marital satisfaction is influenced by sexual fulfillment; sexual fulfillment is influenced by warm religious imagery; and warm religious imagery is influenced by childhood experiences. The religious "stories" about a person's life (as in religious imagery) act as a link between childhood family experiences and adult family experiences. The links are modest, we have said, because there are many other factors which impinge on the development of religious imagery, sexual fulfillment and marital satisfaction. Nevertheless, religious images do precisely what our theory suggests they would do: they are the "stories" which link the beginning of the story of a person's life in his family of orientation with the middle of his story in the family of procreation and point towards the ending of the story -- an ending, if the warm religious imagery is to be believed, which will involve a love affair in a garden of paradise and delight. Even if the imagery is wrong, it still makes for happier marriages (and one will leave to the philosophers and theologians whether such a pragmatic conclusion is evidence for truthfulness of the stories contained in the religious imagery).

I have noted repeatedly that the path of decline and rebirth of marital happiness is paralleled by a decline and rebirth in religious attitudes, images and behaviors. We now must draw this analysis towards a conclusion and ask whether one decline can account for the other. Does a theoretically stated and empirically validated model presented in Table 3.2 account for the decline and subsequent increase in sexual fulfillment and marital satisfaction during the first decade of marriages of young Catholics?

This question can be answered by using a technique of multiple regression analysis called "residual" analysis. The present report is not the place to explain it in any great detail.

It is sufficient to say that one endeavors to diminish percentage point differences by taking into account the influence of variables which are hypothesized as being accountable for the difference. Thus, for example, one finds 50 percentage points difference between Catholics and Jews in the amount of alcohol consumed at a give sitting, and one hypothesizes this difference as a result of mother's and father's drinking behavior. One first mathematically elim- inates the impact of the father and then the impact of the mother (or vice versa) and sees how much the difference between the two ethnic groups drinking has been

diminished. If when the mother's drinking behavior is put into the regression

equation the residual percentage diminishes from 50 to 30, then one can say

that two-fifths of the difference between Irish and Jews in drinking is accounted

for by the fact that Irish mothers drink more than Jewish mothers. If another

ten percentage points decrease occurs when the father's influence is included

in the regression equation, then one can say that the joint influence of mother

and father diminishes the difference by 30 percentage points, and thus "explains"

three-fifths of the difference between the Irish and the Jewish in drinking and

leaves two-fifths difference unexplained by a model which takes into account

only maternal and paternal drinking.

In Table 4.14 a similar technique is used to account for the decline in

13 percentage points on the joint agreement by spouses that their sexual

fulfillment is "excellent" between the first two years of marriage

and the middle years of marriage. The difference declines by 3 percentage

points when one takes into account childhood relationships. Since childhood

relationships have long since been accomplished, one suspects that this .23

explanation of the difference is largely a reconsideration and a reevaluation

of the childhood experience (assuming as we are our cross-sectional analysis

can be considered longitudinal).   Much greater explanatory power

is added to the model when religious imagery is taken into account. The

difference is diminished to 7 percentage points and half of the decline in

sexual fulfillment has been accounted for by a combination of warm religious

imagery and childhood experience. Since the childhood experience is all

reflected through religious imagery, one can say that about one-half of the

decline in sexual fulfillment in young Catholic marriages can be attributable

to the decline in the middle years of the marriage of their warm religious intimacy. Finally, when the ability to express love and affection is taken into account, the difference is reduced by two percentage points and almost two-thirds decline in sexual fulfillment in the young Catholic marriage has been accounted for.

Precisely the same pattern may be observed in explaining the increase in sexual fulfillment between the middle years and the ninth and tenth years of the marriage. In this critical turning point, the level of sexual satisfaction goes up 21 percentage points and more than three-fifths of that increase can be accounted for by family experience and warm religious imagery (the latter of which is indeed the funnel for childhood experiences). (Table 4.15)

In the process of working out the sexual problems in the middle years of the first decade of marriage, Catholic spouses -- in all likelihood, quite unselfconsciously -- are powerfully influenced by a dramatic resurgence in the climate of warm religious imagery in their family. As we have said before, doubtless the causality is reciprocal. The increase in sexual fulfillment is sacramental and revelatory and gives the couple greater confidence in the loving warmth of God. On the other hand, the loving warmth of God seems also to give them greater confidence, to strive for stronger, better sexual intimacy.

Clearly top research priority ought to be to study the crisis which occurs between the middle and the end of the first decade of a Catholic marriage and to sort out the intricate relationship between religious imagery and sexual fulfillment. Presently we must be content to say that it seems more likely that the changing image of God influences changing marital satisfaction than vice versa. But still both doubtless influence one another.

A four variable model, adding sexual fulfillment to ability to express

love and affection, religious imagery, and childhood experiences, can be applied

to the decline and resurgence of marital satisfaction (Tables 4.16 and 4.17).

Marital satisfaction declines from the first to the eighth year of marriage by

some 19 percentage points. Most of the explanatory power of our model is con-

tributed by the decline in warm religious imagery and by the decline in the

capacity to express love and affection; together with childhood experiences

these variables explain two-thirds of the decline, and sexual fulfillment, as such,

when added to the model, attributes no further explanatory power. However, as

can be remembered from Figure 4.1, both the ability to express love and affection

and religious imagery and childhood experience are all funneled through sexual

fulfillment. The decline in sexual fulfillment is not the "cause" of the

decline in marital satisfaction, it is the conduit through which these prior

causes work.

The same model explains 55% of the 20 percentage points increase in marital

satisfaction from the eighth to the tenth year of marriage (Table 4.27) -- a highly

successful effort in most social analysis. Again the principal explanatory variables

in the resurgence of marital satisfaction are the increase in the warmth of reli-

gious imagery and the increase in confidence of one's ability to express love and

affection. These factors, plus the childhood experience variable, are channeled

to marital satisfaction through their impact on sexual fulfillment.

Religious imagery, then, plays an extraordinarily important part in the

decline and rebirth of marital happiness, directly influences and channels

childhood experiences toward decline and rebirth of sexual fulfillment in

marriage, and it in turn operates through its impact on the ability to love and sexual fulfillment on marital satisfaction in the Catholic family. To summarize the model, warm families of origin produce warm religious imagery which inturn produces warm sexuality which in turn produces warm marriages. The decline of religious imagery, the decline of sexual fulfillment account for most of the decline in general marital satisfaction, and also the rebirth of religious warmth, sexual warmth, and love warmth leads at the end of the first decade of marriage to a rebirth of marital satisfaction.

Minimally, the reader who may have been skeptical about the impact of religious imagery on sexuality and marital satisfaction can see that an evaluation of the impact of the religious imagery on human life and especially human marital life is in order.

To test the eighth hypothesis presented at the beginning of this chapter, sixty-four percent of those who have had intense religious experiences often or sometimes describe their sexual fulfillment as excellent as opposed to 43 percent who have had these experiences rarely or never -- a statistically significant difference (In Table 4.23 we are reporting not on families but on individual respondents since there are no families made up of two ecstatics). Furthermore, those who have had religious experiences are 20 percentage points more likely to think of God as a lover (an interesting result of having been in the presence of an "overwhelming power which seemed to lift you out of yourself"). The question then arises as to whether it is precisely among those ecstatics who experience God as a lover that there is the greatest likelihood reporting excellent sexual fulfillment in marriage. If such should be the case then the proposition eight as presented in Table 4.2 is validated.

And indeed, as Table 4.23C shows, it is precisely among those who both think of God as a lover and who have had religious experiences often or sometimes.

Sixty-nine percent of those who have had religious experiences and think of God as lover report their sexual fulfillment as "excellent" as opposed to 48 percent of those who have had similar experiences and do not think of God as lover. Religious experience, in other words, helps your sexual fulfillment only if it makes you more likely to think of God as a lover.

EXCURSUS 4A

If there are "warm" scales, are there also "cold" scales? To have a low score on the warm scale merely means that one is "not warm" -- not likely to invest cosmic symbols with warm, loving, delightful attributes. Is there also an image "syndrome" which scores high on explicitly "cold" or "distant" religious imagery?

There is indeed a propensity for some husbands and wives to be high on a factor measuring description by both partners of Jesus and Mary as "distant". This scale correlates (Figure 5B.1) negatively with both marital adjustment and sexual fulfillment and correlates with the respondent coming from a family where religious "joy" was low.

When both the warm and cold image scales are put into a path model (Figure 5.7) an interesting phenomenon occurs: the "cold" images have no direct influence on sexual fulfillment but rather directly affect marital satisfaction while the warm images continue to operate through their impact on sexual adjustment (the two scales correlate negatively with one another -.38). Thinking of Mary and Jesus as distant, in other words, does not lead to a decline in the sexual fulfillment of marital intimacy but thinking of them as warm does increase sexual fulfillment.

The "cold" scale varies strikingly with the marital cycle during the first decade of a marriage (Table 5B.2). A newly married couple is less likely to have a "cold" image of the cosmic symbols. In the middle years of the first decade of marriage the likelihood of such imagery increases and then declines again sharply as the first decade of marriage ends. The combination of the two image configurations accounts for almost half of the rise in marital satisfaction at the end of the decade (Table 5B.3) and almost 2/3 of the increase in sexual fulfillment. We again are unable to sort out the mutual influences of imagery and marital adjustment.

Summary

1) Family experiences in childhood affect religious images of an adult and through that imagery marital happiness. The warmer the childhood, the "warmer" the religious imagery.

2) Warm religious imagery in turn affects both the capacity to express love and the capacity for sexual fulfillment. The warmer the religious imagery of husband and wife (as expressed in a joint measure), the more likely they are to describe a "warm" (i.e. "excellent") situation in their family with regard to both sexual fulfillment and capacity for loving.

3) In turn marital satisfaction (both "very satisfied") is to a considerable extent shaped by "warm" religious imagery and "warm" sexual fulfillment.

4) As a marriage develops there are stronger correlations between the wife's religious imagery and the husband's religious imagery.

5) Much of the decline in sexual fulfillment and its subsequent rise are explainable by a model which takes into account family "warmth," religious "warmth," and the perceived capacity to love.

6) Much of the decline in marital satisfaction and its subsequent rise are explainable by a model which takes into account family "warmth," religious "warmth," the perceived quality to love, and sexual fulfillment.

7) Religious warmth and sexual fulfillment are the critical variables in the rebound of marriages at the end of their first decade.

8) Those who have intense religious experiences have warmer religious imagery and, hence, more satisfying marriages.

9) There are "cold" as well as warm religious images; the former have the

opposite effect on marital adjustment than the effect of the latter, correlating with low levels of sexual adjustment and marital satisfaction when both husband and wife are high on the "cold" scale. A combination of the sets of images explains a substantial proportion of the dramatic increase in marital adjustment at the end of the first decade of marriage.

Chapter Five - Religious Life Cycle, Marriage and Religious Imagery

In the Knights of Columbus preliminary report, my colleagues and I
discovered that the religious behavior of young American Catholics goes
through a "u curve" during the decadent 20's, decling dramatically from the
early to the middle 20's and then rebounding sharply -- though not to
previous levels -- in the late 20's. This age cycle of religious devotion
seems to so closely parallel the cycle of marital satisfaction described
previously that it seems safe to assume as a working hypothesis that the
two phenomona are related if not identical. In my attempt to explain the
religious life cycle then, I propose the following specific hypotheses:

1) Decline of religious devotion of American Catholics is a form
   of institutional "alienation"; a partial withdrawal of affiliation
   from the institutional church which parallels a withdrawal from
   other institutions in society.

2) Given the enormous disagreement between the attitudes on sexual
   matters of young Catholics and the teachings of the institutional
   church, it is hypothesized that a strong contributor to the
   institutional disaffiliation will be the attitudes of young Catholics
   on premarital sex and on living together before marriage.

3) Given what we have seen in the previous chapters about the relationship
   between marriage and religious devotion, it is hypothesized that a
   substantial part of the rebound phenomenon will be explainable in
   terms of marriage reintegrating young people into social institutions,
   and in particular into the church. A marriage between two Catholics,
   and especially a marriage to a devout spouse, will facilitate this
   reintegration.

4) "Warm" religious imagery will in part cancel the effect of attitudes
   of sexual permissiveness and the increase of shared warm religious
   imagery in a marriage will reduce even more the effect of attitudes
   of sexual permissiveness.

The last point is worth dwelling on because it is a theoretical proposition
derived from the perspective on religion laid out in the previous chapter: warm
images of the Cosmic Powers combined with, reinforced by, and reinforcing a warm
marital relationship will tend to reduce the effect of attitudes supportive of
sexual promiscuity and sexual intimacy without public commitment.

Note well that the expectation described in the previous paragraph runs
strongly against the conventional wisdom. First of all, it would seem unlikely
that a young person's images of God and of Mary and of the afterlife would have
much, if any, effect on his approach to premarital sex; not in a "pagan",
"hedonistic", and secularist society like our own. Secondly, if one were to
expect any influence at all, one might well think it reasonable that someone
who believes that God is a lover and that heaven is a paradise of pleasure and
delight would also think that there is nothing wrong with the delightful
pleasures of love in this life being enjoyed whenever and whereever possible.
That warm religious imagery, in other words, which in the last chapter was
demonstrated to promote sexual fulfillment in marriage would also reasonably
be expected to promote sexual freedom before marriage.

Nonetheless, I am hypothesizing the opposite phenomena. "Stories" implicit
in the "warm" religious images are stories of fidelity, commitment, promises
made, honored, and kept permanently. I therefore predict a negative correlation
between warm images and attitudes of sexual permissiveness - even though such a

prediction may seem to some readers to be absurd. At least, unlike other
pontifications about youthful sex, mine can be tested immediately.

And if mine is right -- be it noted -- the best way the Church can deal
with permissive sexual attitudes about young people is not railing against
the attitudes, not denouncing the behavior as sinful, but preaching ever more
vigorously the warmth and love of God.

In both the United States and Canada, there is a sharp decline from the
middle teen years to the middle 20's in religious devotion (as measured by a
scale composed of prayer, mass attendance, and the reception of communion).
In the United States, 64 percent of those between 14 and 18 are high on this
scale, while those in their later 20's (between 26 and 28) only place 22
percent high on that scale. In Canada the decline is from 53 to 19 percent.
In both countries the enormous decline in religious devotion during the 20's
is statistically significant -- and the average level of such devotion is
significantly higher in the United States than it is in Canada.

In both countries there is a modest rebound of religious activity in the
late 20's; from 22 to 29 percent in the United States and from 19 to 25 percent
in Canada. When the religious resurgence in the two countries is combined, it is
possible to say that the religious revival which seems to occur at the end of
the decade of the 20's (bringing young people back to approximately the level
of religious devotion in their early 20's) represents a significant upward
change of young Catholic religious behavior in North America (North of the Rio
Grande, that is).

In the United States the cycle is at work for both men and women.
Women are more devout than men and their cycle is approximately 10 percentage

points higher than that of the men, starting out at 69 percent, declining at 27 percent, and rebounding to 34 percent; while men begin at 60, decline to 17, and bounce back to 22 percent.

However, in Canada the rebound is limited to women whose proportion high on the religious devotion scale moves from 23 to 34 percent during the last years of their 20's, though no such change occurs in their male counterparts.

It appears that in Canada the religious life cycle rebound is much sharper for English speaking Canadians than for French speaking Canadians. The latter's level of religious devotion increases from 19 to 23 percent while English Canadians' practice rebounds from 16 to 32 percent. The figures for the French Canadians are statistically significant, though not for the English Canadians because of the much smaller sample of English Canadians.

Finally (Table 5.4), it is only the French Canadian males who do not experience a religious resurgence in the last years of the 20's -- though the limited number of cases makes this finding both very tentative and impossible to explain.

The decline and then partial rise of religious devotion among young Catholics in their 20's seems then to be a phenomenon which is not limited within one national culture. Three different cultural groups -- Catholics in the United States, French speaking Canadian Catholics, and English speaking Canadian Catholics -- all seem to experience the phenomenon. Young people "drift" dramatically away from religion during their middle 20's and then, somewhat less dramatically, seem to "drift" back.

Figure 5.1 is a graphic presentation of the first three hypotheses stated at the beginning of this chapter. Sexual permissiveness is measured by a scale

composed of attitudes towards living together before marriage and premarital
sex. Alienation from the church is measured by questions asking the respondents
to place himself/herself on a five-point scale indicating how close or how far
he/she feels from the church. Organizational alienation is based on a factor
created from the items in question 23 (Appendix A). The item on confidence in
organized religion is omitted from the scale. A spouse is considered Catholic
if the spouse's present religious affiliation is Catholic and the distinction
is between married and "non-married" so that the latter includes widowed,
divorced, separated and those living together without benefit of wedlock.

In Figures 2 and 3 this model is applied to religious practice in the
United States and Canada. In both countries the R is about .5, meaning that
approximately one quarter of devotional and religious practice can be
explained by the model. In the United States religious practice is influenced
directly by the religion of one's spouse, alienation from the church and
sexual permissiveness. Alienation from the church, in its turn, is directly
influenced by spouse's religion, sexual permissiveness and organizational
alienation. Sexual permissiveness and organizational alienation are both
influenced by whether one is married or not. Marriage, then, in the United
States, seems to produce a higher level of opposition to sexual permissiveness
and a greater degree of confidence in the organizational and institutional
structures of the society. Young people go through a dramatic period of
alienation in their twenties, turning off all social institutions including
the church. However, when they "settle down" and begin a family of their own,
they become both more hostile of permissiveness and more confident of the
organizational structures of the society. Marriage, apparently, reintegrates
them into the society and also into the church -- especially in the latter
case if the spouse is Catholic.

There are only minor differences between the model for the U.S.A. and for Canada (Figure 5.3). There is no direct linkage between having a Catholic spouse and religious practice in Canada. The spouse's influence is indirect. If you marry a Catholic in Canada, you are less likely to be alienated both from the general social institutions and also from the church. However, in Canada, the mere fact of being married does not diminish organizational alienation.

So our hypothetical model does indeed explain a satisfactory amount of the variance in religious devotion in both countries being studied. The question now becomes whether permissiveness and alienation change as young people grow older and whether this change can account for the change in their religious behavior. Sexual permissiveness is higher in Canada than in the United States (Tables 5.5 and 5.6) though Canadian Catholics are somewhat less likely to be alienated from their church than are American Catholics. On the other hand, organizational alienation is much higher in Canada than in the United States principally because of greater Canadian skepticism over those running the legal system, organized labor, education, major companies and the banks. At least all three items varied by age in both countries (Tables 5.7 to 5.9). Note that in these tables, these scores represent a measure of variation from the mean for the individual country and hence are not comparable across columns. One should, merely inspect each column to see whether in both countries there is a pattern parallel to the religious life cycle described previously. In the United States, all three scales follow the expected change with both permissiveness and the two kinds of alienation increasing in the early and middle 20's and then decreasing in the later 20's. There is little change in attitudes towards sexual permissiveness in Canada in the late 20's though both organizational and ecclesiastical alienation decrease as young people approach thirty.

In Table 5.10 we can compare the relative impact of these variables on religious behavior in a way that might not have been possible from looking at the two flow charts. There is relatively little difference between the correlations in the two countries. While the Catholicism of the spouse is more important in the United States than in Canada, the sexual permissiveness factor is somewhat more powerful in Canada than in the United States. However, when one looks at those who are unmarried (Table 5.11) one can see that there is virtually no difference in the effect of organizational alienation, sexual permissiveness, and closeness to the church on religious devotion.

I now propose to use the same technique of "residual analysis" used in previous chapters to see if the variables in our model can account for much of the religious life cycle -- both the decline from the early to the middle 20's and then the rise at the end of the late 20's. A hint of what the results will be, however, can be found in Table 5.12 where we look at religious devotion for "non-marrieds" in both countries under study. There is no rise at all in religious devotion at the end of the 20's for those who are not married. It would, therefore, appear that the rise in the religious devotion among young Catholics who are between 29 and 30 years old is almost entirely a function of the fact that more than that age are likely to be married and that married peoples' religious devotion is higher than that of single people.

Figures in Tables 5.13 and 5.14 confirm this expectation. By merely taking into account marriage and the religiousness of spouse one can account for almost nine-tenths of the 26 percentage points difference on the religious devotion scale between those in their early 20's and those between 26 and 28 in the United States. In Canada, two-thirds of the 21 percentage points difference can also be explained. In other words, those in their early and middle 20's who are married do not experience the sharp decline in religious practice that singles experience, particularly if they are married to Catholics. Marriage, and especially a marriage to a Catholic, reintegrates them into the social structure of the country and into the organizational structure of the church.

Similarly, almost nine-tenths of the rebound in the United States and half of the rebound in Canada can be accounted for by factors related to marriage. The apparent religious life cycle is in fact part of a larger life cycle. Those who are married are more likely to be religious than those who are not, presumably because marriage, particularly to one of the same faith, puts higher value on social and institutional integration.

Marriage, in other words, cancels the alienation that goes on among the "non-married". All of the 16 percentage points decline in religious devotion among the "non-marrieds" from the beginning to the end of a decade of the 20's in Canada can be accounted for by organizational alienation, sexual permissiveness, and alienation from the church; while three-fifths of the decline among the "non-marrieds" in the United States (a much larger decline because Catholics in the United States in their early 20's are much more devout than Catholics in Canada in their early 20's) can be accounted for by the same model. The decade of the 20's is a time of alienation from social institutions and from the church; an alienation which, in both countries, is reinforced and strengthened by the conflict between young peoples' sexual attitudes and the sexual attitudes of the church. Marriage seems to cancel out much of this alienation and to account

entirely for the rebound.[4]

The dynamics of the religious life cycle are now clear. Religious behavior

goes up in the late 20's because more people are married in their late 20's

(Table 5.16). Sixty-nine percent of Catholics between 22 and 25 are not

---

[4]This report is not the place to discuss in any great detail materials from
the history of the family and the ebb and flow of sexual permissiveness,and from
the history of the church and the requirement that the parish priest witness
solemnly the sexual union in order that it might be "valid". It suffices to
say on the former subject that there are two principal schools in the exciting
new discipline of the history of the family (or demographic history) on the
subject of sexual permissiveness. One school offers considerable evidence that
later middle ages/early modern era were times of tight sexual control by family
and community on the lives of young people. However, in the 1700's and early
1800's this communal control broke down (if there really was ever a major
sexual revolution, it occurred then). Such a change, it is argued, was a single
one-directional event and the result of changing attitudes about the nature of
human freedom. The other position argues that sexual restrictiveness and
sexual permissiveness tend to alternate one with each other in complicated cycles
depending on economic conditions -- particularly as they are affected by plagues,
blights, harvests, increase of trade, and industry, among other factors. Permissiveness, from this point of view, goes with affluence. While the evidence
in family histories shifts backwards and forwards as new discoveries are made
in obscure archives around the western world, it now seems that the better
evidence is on the side of the second position. While economic affluence does
not automatically "cause" permissiveness, they do seem to go hand in hand.
Similarly, the requirement of a public church ceremony to validate a marital
union was applied to the universal church only in the document Tametsi from the
Council of Trent. Even this document was not applied universally. So that
before Trent in many places,and after Trent in some places (until the promulgation
of the new code of canon law in the early part of the 20th century), the so-called
common law union, or its equivalent in non-Anglo Saxon legal systems, was
considered a valid marriage. Professor Natalie Zemon Davis explains the
social and economic reasons for the pulmigation of the Tametsi -- according to the
author (not a Catholic) a much more moderate response demands parents to exercise
control over the marriage of their children than were the responses of Protestant
denominations.
This comment is not meant to suggest that the present requirements for a
church marriage ought to be changed. It is merely an observation that for much
of christian history, common law marriages or their equivalent would not have
been met with grave disfavor in the church, nor are they today in many Latin
American countries.
The observations in this note are not to be taken as evidence that I approve
of premarital sex as it is currently practiced in the United States. On spiritual,
ethical and psychological grounds, I do not.

married, and 44 percent of those between 26 and 28 are not married; while the proportion of Catholic marriages increases from 17 percent of those between 22 and 25 to 46 percent of those between 29 and 30 (could it be that those Catholics who wait longer to get married are more likely to marry other Catholics? There is no change in the proportion of the population that are in mixed marriages after the age of 26. It may also be, however, that young Catholics feel freer to enter religiously mixed marriages or that there are a higher number of converts among the spouses of Catholics in their late 20's).

Similarly, in both the United States and Canada, there is also an increase in the devotion of married people as they get somewhat older and perhaps begin to work out a joint family approach to religion. Thus, not only are people in their late 20's more likely to be married, but those married people in their late 20's are also more likely to be devout. Note especially in Table 5.17 that entering a religiously mixed marriage does not seem to make all that much difference in the devotion of a Catholic. Among those between 29 and 30, 18 percent of the "non-marrieds" are high on the religious devotion scale, 20 percent of the Catholics in mixed marriages, and 46 percent of Catholics in Catholic marriages.

We have answered the question of why married people are more likely to be devout than single people: they are less alienated, though if they are in a religiously mixed marriage they are not much less alienated from the church. Two remaining questions must be answered: what goes on in a Catholic marriage that leads to a resurgence of religious devotion and why do some Catholics choose to marry other Catholics and some choose to marry non-Catholics.

Table 5.19 shows that approximately one-half of the 55 percentage points difference in religious devotion between the two kinds of Catholic marriages can be accounted for by the model, and more than half of that half by the fact that in devout Catholic marriages the husband and wife share warm religious images. It is precisely the "stories of God" which husband and wife have worked out together play a major share in explaining why they are devout and their counterparts who do not have these stories are not devout. As we can observe in Table 5.21, the model is most successful in explaining the differences between the two kinds of Catholic marriages in the key age group of those between 29 and 30. The 59 percentage point difference can be dealt with by our explanatory model -- more than three-fifths of the variance.

Furthermore (Table 5.22), warm religious images also account for half of the differences in alienation from the Church between those who are high on the permissiveness scale and those who are low. Permissive young Catholics are 16 percentage points more likely to be alienated from the church than non-permissive and this can be attributed to the fact that the non-permissive share warmer "stories of God".

The impact of images of God on devotion, permissiveness, and alienation can also be presented in percentage form (Tables 5.22 to 5.28). Forty-five percent of those who have warm images are high on the religious devotion scale as opposed to 27 percent of those who do not have such images, and the highest proportion of devout Catholics can be found among those who have both devout spouses and joint warm imagery -- 78 percent of those with devout spouses and warm imagery are themselves high on the religious devotion scale as opposed to 58 percent of those who have devout spouses but who lack warm "stories of God". It is a help, of course, if your spouse is devout but the help is much greater (and "significantly" greater) if you also share common "warm religious imagery".

Figure 5.4 introduces religious images into our discussion of the former question. It hypothesizes that warm religious images will have an effect on both permissive attitudes and the feeling of alienation from the church and, hence, affect the levels of religious devotion in Catholic marriages. If a couple shares warm "stories of God", they will be more opposed to permissiveness, less alienated from the church, and hence more devout. Figure 5.5 demonstrates this, the most controversial hypothesis stated at the beginning of the present chapter. Religious imagery does indeed diminish both permissiveness and alienation. Those who have warm stories of God in their creative imagination are more opposed to premarital sex and living together than those who do not, and are also likely to feel less alienated from the church. In families where couples share these warm religious images there will be less support for permissiveness, less feeling of alienation and greater religious devotion.

We must now determine who these warm religious images work in Catholic marriages to "de-alienate" Catholic young people. First of all (Table 5.18), high levels of religious practice in Catholic marriages are only to be found when both the respondent and the spouse are high on the religious devotion scale. There is virtually no difference between those in religiously mixed marriages and those who do not have a devout spouse in their own religious devotion. Indeed, of the 29 and 30 year level, those in mixed marriages seem more devout than those in Catholic marriages without a devout spouse. In those marriages where the spouse is devout, the respondent's level of religious devotion declines from 81 to 67 percent between the early and middle 20's, but then bounces back to 72 percent in the late 20's. Can the model presented in Figure 5.5 explain some of the differences in religious devotion between those Catholics who have devout spouses and those who do not?

A third of those with warm images describe themselves as close to the church, significantly different from one fifth of those who do not have warm images (Table 5.25). Furthermore, there is not a statistically significant difference in alienation between those who are more permissive and those who are less permissive if they have warm images. It is only among those who lack such images that the more permissive are statistically more likely to be alienated. Indeed, those who have high permissive attitudes and warm images are as likely to be close to the church as those who have low permissive attitudes but lack the warm images. Imagery, in other words, seems to cancel out the relationship between permissive sexual attitudes and alienation from the church. Warm religious images not only lead to a decrease in sexual permissiveness but they also seem to eliminate the relationship between permissiveness and alienation.

Warm stories of God do not eliminate, by any means, the propensity of young people to be tolerant of sexual permissiveness (Tables 5.27 and 5.28) but they do diminish it substantially. Eighty-four percent of the people in marriages where the spouses do not have a common warm story of God are high on the permissive scale as opposed to 57 percent of those whose family have developed a mutual warm religious imagery. Forty-three percent of those with warm images think that living together is wrong as opposed to 17 percent who lack such images. However, there is virtually no difference between the two groups in their attitudes on birth control.

The stories of God that a husband and wife share, then, play an important part in the modest religious revival which occurs at the end of the late 20's, especially because these images have a notable impact on that group from which the religious "revivalists" are most likely to come, marriages

in which both partners are Catholic. If the church is interested in facilitating

this religious revival and diminishing the levels of alienation from the church

and in contending against sexual permissiveness, the most effective way of doing

so on the basis of the data presently available to them would be to reinforce

as strongly as it can the stories of Jesus and Mary as warm, of God as lover,

and of heaven as a paradise of pleasure and delight.

If we could account for other effective processes by which Catholic marriages

produce greater levels of religious devotion, we are much less successful in

explaining the mixed marriage phenomenon (earlier attempts at explaining

religiously mixed marriages were also unsatisfactory; see Greeley, Crisis in

the Church, 1979.). Only four variables relate at statistically significant

levels to mixed marriages (Table 5.29): poor relationship between parents

when a respondent was growing up; being a child of a religiously mixed marriage;

Catholic education; and warm religious images (of the respondent, not of the

family) (Table 5.25). However, the multiple R of the model presented in Figure

5.6 is only 22, meaning that less than 5 percent of the variance in marital

choice can be accounted for. It would appear that only longitudinal research

in which young people are followed through the life cycle as they make their

marriage choices would offer an explanation why one young Catholic chooses a

Catholic spouse and another does not.[5]

Marriage adjustment then and religious life cycle are both powerfully and

importantly affected by a person's religious images, and in particular by the

joint religious images that a husband and wife share. These images do not

---

[5]It is worth noting, by the way, that there is absolutely no relationship between attendance at Catholic schools and warm images of Cosmic Powers. No matter how many years you have attended Catholic schools you are no more likely to think of God as a lover, heaven as a paradise of delight, or Jesus and Mary as warm than if you did not attend Catholic schools at all -- a somewhat dismaying and disturbing finding for the partisans of Catholic education, who otherwise will find much to console themselves in the present NORC research.

explain the whole of marital satisfaction or the whole of the religious revival

which seems to occur in the late 20's. No one could reasonably expect that they

would, for human behavior, particularly behavior as complex as religious devotion

and marital relationships, is affected by a variety of biological, cultural,

educational, biographical and psychological factors -- as well as, of course,

by free human choice. Still, religious imagery plays a role, an important

role, and indeed, in the religious revival at the end of the 20's, a very

important role indeed, particularly the common religious imagery that a

husband and wife share. These images present an aspect of the church's

doctrine which can be reinforced and emphasized with relative ease and promise

a very substantial payoff both in binding married people more tightly together

and satisfying relationships, and in leading the alienated and disaffiliated

back into the church.

There is a complex, intricate process by which husbands and wives work out,

perhaps implicitly, a common religious posture in the first decade of their

marriage. The posture is affected by their past experiences and affects

many of their present attitudes and behaviors, and will, doubtless, shape

their future. It is the formation of a family religious "stance" that is

intimately affected by and intimately affects the general satisfaction of

their relationship, even though they themselves do not seem to perceive

this because the process is so subtle and complex. In this report I have

been able to describe some of the dynamics which seem to be at work, dynamics

which may seem to many readers to be very intricate and complex. In fact,

my models are much too simple and the reality of husband/wife interactions

as they resolve their problems and fashion a religious story which is no

longer "yours and mine" but "ours" is infinitely more complex than the models I have laid out in the last two chapters. The present report is merely the beginning of a study of how "your story" and "my story" converge into "our story" and then profoundly influence every aspect of our lives. I hope the church will be sufficiently interested in the subject to pursue the matter.

EXCURSUS 5A

Other NORC research has indicated a return to religious practice of Catholics in their 30's, particularly those who attended college and those of Irish ethnic background. Therefore, it seemed reasonable to ask whether there was any sign of either decline or rise of religious practice among the respondents in the Study of Catholic Youth. Table A.1 indicates that on all measures there is a sharp decline in religious practice after a person becomes 22 years old. However, at the end of the 20's there is an upturn, and the members of the last three-year age group, for example, are as likely to say they pray several times a week as the youngest respondents. While their mass attendance, communion reception, and closeness to the Church and to the parish have not returned to the levels of their late teens and early 20's, nonetheless, the level of their religious practice increased over the three-year age cohort just beneath them. Furthermore (the bottom half of Table A.1), our respondents seem to be aware of this change in themselves. The people in their late 20's think of themselves as being closer to God than they were five years previously, and those between 28 and 30 think of themselves as being closer to the Church than they were five years previously.

There are two possible explanations for the "U" curve in religious

behavior which seems to occur to young Catholics during their twenties.

It may be an actual "life cycle" phenomenon with some young people manifest-

ing a decline and then a rise in religious practice. Or it may be a

"generational" phenomenon; those Catholics in the late twenties today

may have always been more devout than those in their middle twenties and

those in their middle twenties may also be less devout than those in

their early twenties. There is not then a change of behavior but a

change of personnel in age categories.

The fact that those in their late twenties now seem to be conscious

that they are closer to their parish than they were previously seems

to indicate an authentic life cycle change. Furthermore, the annual

NORC General Social Survey, taken every year, enables us to ask how the

age cohort now turning thirty behaved religiously at earlier points in the

last decade. In the first column of Table A.2 we see that there was

in fact a lower level of religious practice of this cohort in the early

and middle years of the 1970s and a sharp increase in the last two years.

It would appear that Catholics turning thirty at the present time seem

to have experienced a religious crisis or at least a crisis of religious

behavior in their early and middle twenties and are now in the process

of "rebounding" out of that crisis--an authentic life cycle phenomenon

and not a generational change. (Interestingly enough there is no compar-

able cycle for Protestant young people whose "2 or 3 times a month" church

attendance is constant at 36 percent through this phase of their life.

An alternate possibility (and one which seems more reasonable to the NORC research team) is that young Catholics in the present situation in the church go through a period of disillusionment from which many of them recover after a certain period of time. An earlier generation experienced this disillusionment at a somewhat older age in life. But now the disillusionment has "filtered down" into the middle twenties and has ended by the time young people turn thirty.

Summary

1) In both Canada and the United States, and in both English and French Canada, there is a religious life cycle during the 20's in which religious devotion declines and then rebounds.

2) The decline is the result of the alienation of young people from social structures in general, from the ecclesiastical structure in particular, and of disagreement between their sexual beliefs and the sexual teachings of the church.

3) This decline is effectively "cancelled out" by marriage, particularly in the United States by marriage to a Catholic. Such a marriage leads to a decline in alienation and an increase in social integration and a diminishing support for sexual permissiveness.

4) Marriage to another Catholic leads to religious revival only if the spouses work out however implicitly a joint religious posture which emphasizes devotion.

5) In such marriages in particular, the joint religious imagery -- warm "stories of God" -- play a decisive and critical role, diminishing alienation and cancelling permissiveness, and reinforcing the young Catholic's return to religious devotion.[6]

---

[6]On the basis of data available to us we cannot say that children make a

6) The process of religious reintegration that seems to go on in the late
20's, especially among those who are married to devout Catholic spouses,
is intimately related to the process of religious reintegration. Just as
the Catholic church is a net gainer in such reintegration, so is the
Democratic Party; the latter because religious commitment seems to lead
to social commitment and the Democratic Party apparently still appeals
to young Catholics as the party most likely to stand for social
commitment.

7) Warm images of God lead to warm political and social attitudes in young
Catholic families where these images are shared by husband and wife.
The more passionate one's stories of God, the more passionate one's
involvement in the political and social work.

8) The religious life cycle does seem to be an actual life cycle phenomenon
and not a generational difference.

---

contribution to the religious return of the late 20's. There is, in fact,
no correlation between devotion and whether one has children or how many
children one has. It is marriage, particularly marriage to a Catholic,
rather than child-bearing and rearing, that accounts for the late 20's
religious resurgence. It may be, however, that in the 30's the religious
revival noted in Appendix C can be explained by the fact that during those
years children reach an age at which it becomes necessary to hand on a
religious tradition to them.

Chapter Six - Young Catholic Family's Alienation, Religious Images, and
          Social Attitudes

In this brief chapter I will examine the relationship between religious
alienation and political alienation, and inquire whether passionate imagery of
God leads to political commitment. If one has in one's religious imagination
"warm" images of God, would one also be warmly committed to the cause of social
justice?

Again, I must observe that on a priori grounds there would be enormous
skepticism that one's fantasy about God and the afterlife and Jesus and Mary
would have any relationship to one's social behavior. A theory of the sociology
of religion predicting such a relationship would run the risk of being ridiculed
if it did not provide immediate evidence to support its prediction (and after the
fact, it also runs the risk of being told "Oh well, we knew that all along".)

In the analysis reported in <u>Crisis in the Church</u>, it was discovered that
disaffiliation from the church correlates with disaffiliation from the Democratic
Party for Catholics under 30. When one drifts away from the institutions of one's
childhood, it seems, one drifts away from both political party and the church.

This finding was replicated in the present study. Interestingly enough, the
proportion of young Catholics who are politically alienated (have no party
affiliation, not even "weak" ones) decreases as the decade of the 20's progress,
so that 35% of them have no political affiliation in the early 20's and only
27 percent of them are disaffiliated in their later 20's. The principal
beneficiary of political reaffiliation is the Democratic Party which claims 49
percent of the young Catholics in the early 20's and almost 60 percent of them
in their later 20's.

Is this reaffiliation with the Democratic Party a phenomenon that is linked to religious factors? At first this might seem to be a ridiculous question. Why would more religious Catholics be more likely to be Democratics? An appropriate test seemed to be to correlate political disaffiliation and Democratic Party membership with religiousness of spouse to see whether in working out a family religious strategy there is also a propensity to increase commitment to the Democratic Party as well as to decrease political alienation.

Quite surprisingly (at least to me) is the finding presenting in Table 6.2 that only 4 percent of those who describe their spouse as not religious are likely to describe themselves as strong Democrats, while 18 percent of those who say they have a very religious spouse are strong Democrats. "Strong Democrats", in other words, are precisely the beneficiaries of the decline in political aliena-tion (from 39 percent to 26 percent) which is related to having a "very religious" spouse. For Democratic politicians, then, it would be a useful political strategy to see that young Catholics marry devout spouses or more precisely that young Catholic married couples devise a religious strategy for the family which implies devotion because such a strategy will also imply strong affiliation with the Democratic Party.

It also would be wise, apparently, for such Democratic political leaders to see that young Catholics marry other Catholics. In Figure 6.1 we take a segment out of the model presented in 5.1 with political party disaffiliation replacing organizational alienation in the model. Having a Catholic spouse leads to a decrease in political alienation and that decrease in its turn leads to an increase in closeness to the church. The correlation is somewhat lower between political party disaffiliation and closeness to the church than it is between organizational alienation and closeness to the church -- which is why the latter

variable was used in Chapter Five. However, interestingly enough, the two forms
of alienation -- political and organizational -- are not strongly related so
one could have introduced political disaffiliation into the model in the previous
chapter and improved somewhat its explanatory power at the cost of making it
more difficult to read and understand.

More must be said than this, however. Not only is political disaffiliation
a useful substitute for organizational alienation, it also has a direct impact
on religious devotion (Figure 6.2). The disaffiliated politically are less
likely to be religious. Those with political affiliation are more likely to be
religious especially if they are in the oldest age group (29 and 30 years old)
where both political and religious affiliation are increasing. Thus, one can
say not merely that political and religious reaffiliation go on simultaneously
but that they go on as part of the same process and that the process is
facilitated when one Catholic marries another Catholic.

A striking way of presenting this phenomenon is to look at the relationship
in Catholic marriages between the frequency of one's spouse's communion and one's
political identification either as a disaffiliate or as a strong Democrat
(Table 6.3). If one's spouse goes to communion often there is a .16 (statistically
significant) positive correlation between being a strong Democrat and .12 negative
correlation with being a political disaffiliate. The more often your spouse goes
to communion, the more likely you are to be a strong Democrat, and the less likely
you are to be politically disaffiliated.

The frequency with which one's spouse receives communion correlates with
one's own commitment to aiding the poor. A commitment to the poor also

correlates with strong Democratic affiliation. Might it be that in the more
devout Catholic families, a commitment to the poor is precisely what mediates
between religious devotion and strong attachment to the Democratic party.
Figures 6.4 and 6.5 suggest that this is the case. The positive correlations
between spouse's communion and Democratic affiliation on the one hand, and the
negative correlations between spouse's communion and political disaffiliation
on the other, are both reduced to statistical insignificance (indicated by the
dotted line) when a commitment to aid to the poor is introduced into the
relationship. More devout Catholic families are more likely to be strong
Democrats apparently because they have a stronger commitment to social justice.

The relationship between devotion and commitment to social justice will be
a matter of some joy, doubtless, to church administrators and religious thinkers.
There may be some hesitation, however, to identify the cause of social justice
with the Democratic Party. I do not propose myself to suggest in this report
that such a link represents an accurate reading of political reality. However,
the evidence shows that it is the reading of political reality made by devout
young Catholic families.

Do religious images correlate with social justice commitment as well as
religious devotion? Do warm stories of God tend to support and reinforce (and
be reinforced by) warm religious commitments? Tables 6.4 and 6.5 indicate that
they do indeed. There are significant correlations between warm religious images
and commitment to the cause of racial justice, to aiding the poor and to working on
social problems, and a negative relationship between such images and political
disaffiliation.

Liberals that they may be on social issues, those with warm religious images are significantly more likely to reject so-called "liberalism" on matters of abortion and mercy killing; although there is no significant relationship between such imagery on either the number of children a family has or what it takes to be an ideal number of children. Those young Catholic families, in other words, where there is a strong propensity for husband and wife to think of Jesus and Mary as "Warm," of God as a lover, and of heaven as a paradise of pleasure and delight, are more committed to social justice and more opposed to abortion and mercy killing than are other Catholics, although there is little difference between them and others on the question of family size.

The powerful relationship between religious imagery and social commitment can also be perceived in Table 6.5. Those that are low on the individual warm image scale are half as likely (twenty-seven percent) as those who are high on the scale (fifty percent) who would also be high on the social commitment scale. If you think of Jesus and Mary as warm and of heaven as a paradise of pleasure and delight and God as a lover, inother words, you are twice as likely to be socially committed as you would be if you had none of these images working powerfully in your imagination.

The same model that explained the negative relationship between Holy Communion reception and political disaffiliation also explains the relationship between the warm religious imagery and the rejection of political alienation (figure 6.6). It is precisely the commitment of young Catholics with warm stories of God in their religious imagination to aiding and assisting the poor that leads them to reject the path of political party disaffiliation. They are committed politically because they are committed socially, and they are committed socially because their stories of God reveal to them God's commitment to us, a phenomenon on which theologians and the religious administrators might want to reflect for a long, long time.

Chapter Seven

In this chapter, I propose to consider two subjects: the origins of warm religious images and the relationship between such imagery and propositional world view.

Thus far I have documented the enormous impact that warm religious images can have on the attitudes and behaviors of members of young Catholic families and have demonstrated that both the family of origin and the family of procreation influence the development of such passionate imagery. But what are some of the other factors which might also lead to the development of warm images? Our theory suggests that they are to some extent the product of our "experiences of grace", our contact with meaning or purpose or the sacred or the Other. The images are "residue" of our experience of grace. It is also possible that the images may be the result of traditional aesthetical practices, spiritual readings, retreat, recollection, spiritual direction, and even, perhaps, sermons. But all these theoretical expectations are tricky. If one should, perhaps, find a correlation between the respondent's perception of the quality of sermons that he hears on Sunday and his warm religious images, there are at least four possible explanations for the correlation:

1) High quality sermons improve the religious imagery of Catholics.

2) Those with warm religious images are likely to be more charitable in their judgments about sermons.

3) Those with warm images in their creative preconscious are able to get more out of sermons than those who do not have such images.

4) The person whose creative imagination is possessed by passionate pictures of the cosmic symbols may seek out better preachers.

Any of these four explanations or any combination of them might go into explaining the correlation. Similarly, if there is a relationship between aesthetical practice and religious imagery, that correlation might also be accounted for by explanations parallel to the four just mentioned. Thus, it is possible, on the basis of our theory, to lay out a path model such as the one in Figure 7.1, but the correlation coefficients on the path in the model must be treated with caution. In the absence of much more intricate research, one may only say about the beta coefficients in Figure 7.1 that they represent one of many possible patterns of influence.

It is interesting to note the variables with which warm religious images in an individual do not correlate. The religious images scale does not correlate with Catholic education, with occupation, with income, or with sex. Two ethnic groups, Polish and Hispanic, are somewhat higher on the scale but not high enough to produce a statistically significant correlation. The ordinary demographic predictors, in other words, which are the stock and trade of social science research, have little influence on how the creative imagination pictures Jesus, Mary, God and heaven.

However, as our theory has lead us to suspect (Table 7.1) there are strong and significant correlations between warm religious imagery, the joyousness of the approach to religion in the family background, religious experience, aesthetical practices, the quality of sermons, and the spouse's religiousness. Interestingly enough, the highest correlation is with quality of sermon. As noted previously, one must be very tentative in suggesting which way the causal influence between sermons and religious imagery might go. Nonetheless, religious administrators, pastoral workers, and above all, preachers can hardly afford to take the chance that the quality of the Sunday sermon does not enhance

the religious imagery of many of the people in the congregation.

In a theoretical perspective on which this work is based religious images

are thought of as spontaneous reactions of the creative imagination, or

of the prerational or preconscious personality to experiences of grace,

major and minor. Reflections on these images are, also, religious, but

from the point of view of the theory, secondarily and derivatively religious.

They represent the necessary consideration, explication, formalization

and rationalization of our experiences of grace. My colleague, William

McCready, in a previous work (The Ultimate Values of the American Population,

Sage, 1976.), has developed a technique for measuring basic world view -- the

response of a person to the tragedies, the injustices, and the suffering which

are part of the human condition; the way a person copes with what Paul Ricoeur

calls the "mystery of evil." Such a world view is something more than just

free floating religious imagery and something less than formal catechism or

creed -- though in a sense that it regulates our response to life'c crises,

it may in some ways be more important than creed or catechism. The world view

in which I am interested in this chapter is what McCready calls the "Hopeful

world view," a view which does not run from evil as does an Optimistic view,

nor deny the existence of good as does a Pessimistic view. McCready has

endeavored to measure these world views by presenting respondents with life

situations, vignettes of human tragedy, and asking the respondent which of a

number of possible reactions is most likely to be his/her own. The vignettes

are in questions 31-32 in Appendix A. The Hopeful response is the sixth one to

each vignette. In his research McCready has demonstrated that these world

view patterns relate both to background, variables in a respondent's past, and to his present attitudes and behaviors on such matters as, for example, racial justice. (The more hopeful one is, the more likely one is to be committed to racial integration).

It seems reasonable to assume that warm religious images would contribute to a hopeful world view. Indeed, the concept of measuring religious images was initially developed by McCready and myself to see if we could link more intimately the religious experience of our respondents with the world view. Thus, we predict a correlation between religious experience and warm images, and also a correlation between images and world view.

The correlation coefficients in Table 7.2 demonstrate that our expectations were indeed correct. There is a powerful .37 correlation between warm religious images and a hopeful world view, and all the factors which produce warm images also correlate with a hopeful perspective on tragedy and death -- family religious spirit, religious experience, aestheticism, sermons, and spouse's religiousness.

In Figure 7.1, I present, as a five variable model, one possible flowchart demonstrating the relationships among religious experiences, religious images and hopefulness.

Religious images are shaped by sermons, by aesthetical practice, by religious experience (both directly and through the impact of religious experiences on sermons and aestheticism) and finally by family religious spirit, directly and indirectly through the three intervening variables. We are more likely to have warm religious images if we come from a joyous religious family, have had religious experiences, listen to excellent sermons, and engage in the traditional aesthetical practices.

Furthermore, imagery, religious experience, and family joy all directly influence a hopeful world vision, imagery more powerfully than the other two.

Sermons and aesthetical practices exercise their effect on the hopeful world view only indirectly through their contribution to the growth of religious images, and the direct path of both religious experience and family religious joy is substantially reduced from the simple correlation in Table 7.2. In other words, a substantial part of the impact of family religiousness and religious experience on a hopeful world view is filtered through religious imagery while religious experience and family joy have indeed a direct and independent impact on hopefulness. They also influence hopefulness because they contribute to the creation of positive and of passionate "stories of God". About one-half of the influence of the family flows through religious imagery and about one-third of the influence of religious experience on hopefulness flows through the warm images.

In Figure 7.2, the aesthetical factor is taken out of the model and replaced by spouse's religiousness (hence, only the married respondents are represented in Figure 7.2).[7]

Spouse's religiousness does indeed have a direct influence on hopefulness but it also has an indirect impact through the relationship between spouse's religiousness and warm imagery. The devout spouse inclines you to be both warmer in your religious images and more hopeful, and part of the link between the spouse's religiousness and hopefulness comes through the fact that a devout spouse inclines you to have more positive and passionate pictures of God, Jesus, Mary, and heaven.

Image and world view, then, are indeed intimately linked. Both are shaped by experience; the experience of the family of origin, the experience of the

---

[7]The aesthetical variable is removed for purposes of simplicity of presentation in the model. Both aestheticism and spouse's behavior make independent contributions to the development of warm images.

family of procreation, religious experience, the experience of hearing good sermons, and the experience of traditional aesthetical exercises. Much of the impact of these different kinds of experiences on a hopeful world view is filtered through the religious image, which in our theory precedes the world view in the creative imagination.

The spouse's of our respondents were also asked to rate themselves on McCready's vignette items and so it was possible to see whether husbands and wives tend to have the same kind of world view. In fact, there is a strong .35 correlation between husband's hopefulness and wife's hopefulness (Table 7.3), and this correlation almost doubles from the beginning of the first decade of marriage to the end of the decade (Table 7.3). The two spouses, in other words, converge in their hopefulness (or their lack of hopefulness) as years of their common life lengthen. In the experience of the young Catholic family, in other words, hope feeds on hope and lack of hope feeds on the lack of hope. As might be expected, the family religious imagery contributes to family hopefulness. (Figure 7.3). The correlation between a high score for both husband and wife on the warm image scale and a high score for both on the hopefulness scale is almost .4. If the image environment of the family is high on warmth, then the world view environment of the family is high on hope.

Some readers may be uneasy with the notion that religion exist primordially in the creative imagination and only reflectively in the intellect - even if there is a powerful correlation between the two. However, instead of the words 'creative imagination", one merely uses the word "spirit" -- in the sense of St. Paul's words "The spirit speaks to our spirit" -- then it becomes easier to comprehend the distinction our theoretical perspective is making. The human personality and its "spirit" experiences God's love, his warm and passionate love, through the various sacraments which manifest and reveal that love, especially the sacrament of the family. Then the human rationalizes and analyzes the meaning of that experience and develops a self conscious world view which enables it to cope, hopefully, with tragedy and death. In many cases it seems safe to assume this analysis is not formal or explicit, not an elaborate act of theological abstraction, but a quick leap of religious reflection. If God is a lover, and heaven a paradise of pleasure and delight, why should not one be hopeful, at least moderately, in the face of suffering and tragedy?

EXCURSUS: ORTHODOXY, IMAGERY AND PRAYER

A belief system or a world view is indeed propositional, at least as it
is measured in McCready's method. A world view is a set of responses that a
person has at hand to deal with the problems of good and evil that he encounters
in his life. It is something more than a religious image and something less than
a credal proposition, for it lacks the formal explicit articulation that one
expects in credal propositons. Reflective and propositional, but not formally
precise, the world view presumably is open to influence both by religious images
and by formal doctrinal convictions. The question then arises as to whether
doctrinal convictions are more important, or religious images (stories of God)
are more important in producing a hopeful world view (and for the purpose of
this excursus, a commitment to social action).

An orthodoxy scale was prepared on responses to a number of belief items
(put in belief question) having to do with a respondent's attitude towards
papal primacy, papal infallibility, mass attendance, the existence of the devil,
and the existence of eternal punishment in hell. The models in Figures 7.4 and
7.5 are designed to compare the relative impact of the orthodoxy scale and the
religious imagery on hopefulness and on social commitment (commitment to work on
social problems, to work for racial justice, and to aid the poor). It is clear
that religious images have a far more powerful impact on a hopeful world view
than does doctrinal orthodoxy, though the modest correlation between orthodoxy
and hopefulness (.1) is statistically significant. There is, however, no relationship between doctrinal orthodoxy and social commitment and a significant
relationship between warm religious imagery and social commitment.

If the way one handles tragedy and the way one responds to social problems are measures of desirable religious behavior, it is clear from the two Figures that it is the stories of God and not the doctrinal proposition that motivates desired attitudes and actions. I am not suggesting, of course, that there is no room for credal or catechetic propositions in religion or that doctrinal orthodoxy is unimportant or that no efforts should be made to oversee such orthodoxy. However, the evidence does seem to suggest that important as it may be in its own sphere, it is not orthodoxy which produces either hope or commitment, but rather the "stories of God" contained in passionate religious images, stories of which the orthodox proposition are formal articulation and on which (as on the gospel where the stories are the gospel) orthodoxy depends, if not for its precision, then at least for its driving force.

Finally (Figure 7.6), there is no significant relationship between prayer and orthodoxy but a strong (.28) standardized correlation between warm images and prayer. It's not what you believe which leads you to pray but how you picture God and the other cosmic symbols.

Summary

1) The development of a warm religious imagination is in part the result of experiences -- joyous family of origin, religious experiences, the experience of hearing good sermons, the experience of having a religious spouse, and the experience of traditional aesthetical practices. From the point of view of ecclesiastical policy making, a strong relationship between quality of sermons and warm religious imagery cannot be over-estimated.

2) Warm "stories of God" lead to a hopeful world view, a world view which without denying the existence of evil, still sees goodness as stronger than evil (if on occasion only moderately so). Much of the influence of background experiences on hopefulness is filtered through warm religious images.

3) One may usefully conceptualize the impact of religious experience on the creative imagination by using St. Paul's terminology that "the spirit speaks to our spirit."

4) The hopefulness of one's world view, one's social commitment and one's propensity to frequent prayer are not influenced to any appreciable extent by one's doctrinal orthodoxy, but strongly influenced by one's warm religious imagery.

Chapter Eight - Human Intimacy and Divine Intimacy: An Empirical Test

Christian religious theory has always maintained that there is a link
between human love and divine love. Marriage is, according to St. Paul, a
"great sacrament," that is to say, a "revelation" of God's love for His
people. As husband and wife love one another, so do God and the Church.
Similarly, husband and wife ought in their relationship to try to imitate the
love of God for the Church. The imagery is a two way street: marriage
revealing the passion of God's love for His people, and the generosity of
God's love providing an ideal for the married life. St. Paul himself
frequently gets his syntax confused as he tries to go in opposite directions
on the symbolic street.

In traditional Christian marriage catechesis much has been made of the
relationship between "the two loves." If human spouses love God strongly
it is argued, they will also love one another strongly. Their faith in
God will strengthen their faith in one another, and their love for one another
will motivate them to grow in love of God.

It is often hard to tell how serious this catechesis is taken. Does
the overarching "story" of God's love effect the emerging "story" of "our
love," and does "our" love one for another rebound back to intensify our
involvement in God's story?

Does divine intimacy really affect human intimacy and vice versa? How
closely are the two love stories related? Is the relationship merely a matter
of conventional piety without any measurable impact on people's lives?

If one takes prayer as a fair measure of intimacy with God and sexual
fulfillment as a fair measure of intimacy with one's spouse, it is possible
to fashion a rough and ready empirical test of the nature of the relationship

between the two loves. What effect does the prayer life of a young Catholic married couple have on their sex life? I want to note again that such questions asked in many fashionable and progressive Catholic circles would lead to ridicule. Prayer is nice, one might be told, and sex is nice, but the two really do not mix.

In approximately a quarter of the Catholic marriages we have studied both members of the couple pray every day. In forty-two percent of those families both husband and wife described their sexual fulfillment as "excellent." On the other hand, where one or both of the spouses does not pray every day only twenty-four percent described their sexual fulfillment as "excellent" (Table 8.1). The difference is statistically significant, and the coefficient of association (gamma) is quite high -- .50. Prayer and sex do, indeed, mix, and the two loves do, indeed, relate strongly one to another.

Moreover, the association between husbands' and wives' prayer (Table 8.2) increases with the duration of marriage. The gamma in the early years of marriage is .31. It diminishes to .21 between the third and the eighth year of marriage but then rises to .42 during the last two years of the first decade of marriage. As your story and my story become our story, both of us are more likely to get involved with God (though not necessarily together, since the question merely revealed whether the respondent and the spouse pray every day, and not whether they pray together).

We know from chapter four that there is a correlation between warm images and sexual fulfillment, and we are not surprised (Table 8.3) to see that those who have warm images of the cosmic personages are also more likely to communicate with them. Hence, prayer, sexual fulfillment and warm religious images intercorrelate with one another. The more a husband and wife pray, the more likely they are to have sexually fulfilling marriages,

and the warmer the imagery, the more likely they are to have sexually
fulfilling marriages. Furthermore, both of these variables, while they
are related to each other, also make an independent contribution to each
other (figure 8.1) to sexual fulfillment. They are not substitutes for one
another. The greatest probability of sexual fulfillment comes in marriages
in which there is both daily prayer by the two spouses and warm images
in the religious fantasy of the two spouses. Indeed, (Table 8.4) it is
precisely among those marriages in which both spouses pray every day and
both spouses have warm images that the difference in sexual fulfillment occurs.
More than half of them report excellent sexual fulfillment (by both husband
and wife), twice as many as in the other three categories. In the technical
parlance of social science, daily prayer specifies the difference in sexual
fulfillment between those families which share warm imagery and those that
do not. It is precisely the combination of the two, in other words, that
accounts for the difference in sexual fulfillment in a young Catholic
family.

The proportion of Catholic families in which both husband and wife
pray every day increases as the marriage goes on (Table 8.5). It is not
merely, then, that "your" story and "my" story become more closely related, and
that "your" story of "your" relationship with God and that "my" story of "my" relationship
with God tend to converge (as we saw in Table 8.2). It is also true that
"our" joint relationship with God improves through the years of the marriage,
just as our relationship with one another is improving. As "our" story gets
better, so does "our" involvement in God's story become more active.

It is impossible, of course, with our present data to sort out the
influence flow between the two loves. St. Paul's difficult syntax as he

shifts back and forth manifests the same problem that the researcher faces: the two loves are so closely connected that it is hard to chart the ebb and flow one upon the other. However, if one pursues the model used in previous chapters (Table 8.6) and assumes at least some influence of prayer and warm images on the changing level of the sexual fulfillment in young Catholic families, one can say that prayer makes an additional contribution to the explanation of the rebound between the middle and late years of marriage and sexual fulfillment. The difference between the third and the eighth year on the one hand and the ninth and the tenth year on the other is, it will be recalled from previous chapters, twenty-two percentage points. When the warm imagery is taken into account the difference diminishes to nine percentage points -- in other words, three-quarters of the increase in sexual fulfillment can be accounted for by changes in the religious imagery of the spouses between the middle and the end of the first decade of their marriage. When one adds to that the daily prayer of spouses the difference diminishes even more to six percentage points, and one has accounted for three-quarters of the change in sexual fulfillment. Whether religion influences sexuality or sexuality influences religion may be hard to determine. That they both have an extraordinary impact on one another is now beyond any doubt.

A final comment is in order about whether the influences described in this book are perceived by the husbands and wives involved. Do men and women know that they are being influenced religiously by their mate? One of the questions in the survey asked the respondent to rate a number of potential religious influences on a four point scale (mother, father, friends, priests, etc.). If correlations exist between the conscious rating of the spouse's influence and the family religious styles analyzed in this report

that it would follow that not all the husband-wife, wife-husband influence

is preconscious or subconscious (about 18% say that their spouse has a

"great deal" of religious influence).

In fact (Table 8.7), there are statistically significant correlations

between the perception of spouse's influence and the joint imagery, joint

prayer and joint sexual fulfillment measures. We cannot say with certainty

that there is a consciousness that the spouse is leading the respondent

to pray more or to have warmer religious imagery, but there is a consciousness

that the spouse is exercising influence.

Furthermore (Table 8.8), this influence seems to wane, then wax during

the first ten years of marriage, as do so many other aspects of the relationship.

In the final years of the decade the spouse's religious influence is more

likely to be perceived as strong than during the earlier years. Also

(Table 8.9), the correlations between imagery and prayer on the one hand

and perceived influence of the spouse on the other seem to go through the

same "U curve;" the relationship between the perception of the spouse's

influence and the joint imagery and joint behavior is strongest during the

final years of the first decade of marriage. Not only do joint prayer

and joint imagery increase in the "rebound" period, so does the perception

of the spouse's influence and the relationship between such a perception

and prayer and imagery. Not only are "your" story and "my" story becoming

"our" story, but "we" are becoming selfconscious about the fact that it is

"our" story.

Figure 8.2 demonstrates one possible influence flow. Husband and wife

have warm religious images. This sharing of "stories of God" makes it more

likely that the two of them will pray frequently. A combination of the "stories" and the mutual (if not common) prayer, leads them to perceive that they are having more religious influence on one another. All three factors improve their sexual fulfillment.

If one adds self consciousness about religious influence to the explanatory model developed to explain the "rebound" in sexual fulfillment, then 75% of the 22% point increase between the 3-8 and the 9-10 year can be accounted for.

Earlier in the chapter it was noted that 52% of those couples both of whom pray every day and both of whom have warm religious images report that their sexual fulfillment is excellent. If one adds selfconsciousness about spouse's influence, the percentage rises to 57% -- 10 percentage points higher than those with images and prayer but without the selfconsciousness and 35 percentage points higher than the rest of the sample (Table 8.10).

Thus, not only is there some selfconsciousness about religious influence of the spouse, but this selfconsciousness heightens the impact of the influence.

Summary

1) Daily prayer by both spouses has an extraordinarily powerful relationship with sexual fulfillment. Those marriages in which both spouses pray every day are almost twice as likely to be marriages in which both spouses say their sexual fulfillment is excellent.

2) When daily prayer is added to warm family religious imagery (with which it correlates) almost three-quarters the rebound in family sexual fulfillment during the final years of the first decade of marriage can be explained.

3) Prayer, sexuality and religious imagery are intimately interconnected. The relationship between the "stories" of two loves, human and divine, has been documented empirically for young Catholic families.

Chapter Nine -- Conclusions & Implications

The following concluding comments seem to be appropriate:

1) Despite the facts that one-third of the young Catholics today are married invalidly and that one-half of them are married to non-Catholics and that most reject the Church's teachings on birth control, divorce, and premarital sex, the young Catholic family seems to have remarkable durability. Most of them do not get divorced and many of them remain together despite what seems to be enormously trying years between the third and the eighth year of the first decade of their marriage. While the Church clearly must minister to "unsuccessful" young Catholic families, it must also realize that there is considerable residual strength and resourcefulness in the typical young Catholic family and that it probably needs encouragement more than either therapy or denunciation.

2) It seems that the young Catholic family (and probably other young American families too) go through a rather long and painful period of adjustment for perhaps five or six years of the first decade of married life. Not all families experience this half decade of turbulence, but the majority seem to and it is safe to say that the typical young Catholic family has a very hard time before it reaches the turning point towards the end of the first decade of marriage. However, the turning point is reached and most young Catholic families, pretty much on the internal residual strength of their relationship, survive the crisis and achieve a level of happiness equal to or indeed in excess of that which marks the beginning of the marriage.

Therefore, in premarriage as well as in marriage instruction, the Church should prepare its young people for this typical, if not universal, crisis and tell them that the crisis can be survived and is survived by most young families and leads to considerable happiness and satisfaction once it has been overcome. People need to know both that they are going to face this crisis and that typically they can face it successfully.

3) The crisis of the middle of the first decade is both religious and sexual and religion and sexuality intermingle in both the decline of marital happiness and then its resurgence; intermingle in such a way that it is virtually impossible to separate one from the other. Religion, in these circumstances, is not merely prayer, church attendance, and belief in the after life (though these things are involved, too). It is religious imagery -- those cosmic pictures or stories by which people represent and rearticulate to themselves what life in general, and their own life in particular, is all about. As the church endeavors to minister to the young Catholic family, it must strive to facilitate the growth and development of "warm" religious imagery and a fulfilling sexual life for young married people. Yet, the church is doing rather little of either. Its sexual catechesis is almost entirely negative and its teaching on God as a lover and heaven as a paradise of pleasure and delight -- to the extent that it exists at all -- has been patently ineffective because most young Catholic married people do not spontaneously think of either image. One need only read the New Testament to see that there the imagery is very warm and

positive, but that is not the way the imagery of Catholicism
is perceived by members of young Catholic families.

4) A religiously mixed marriage simply does not seem to have available
nearly as much in the way of the resources necessary for marital
"rebound" towards the end of the first decade, perhaps because
it is less likely than the Catholic marriage to generate the
atmosphere of "warm" religious imagery which facilitates the rebound
(and whose growth and development is also in turn facilitated
by the rebound).

5) The family is a sacrament (with a small s) -- both the family of
procreation and the family of origin -- because it reveals the
warmth and love of God and the splendors that he has prepared for
us, the link between the sacramentality of these two families is
another set of sacraments (also with a small s) -- the religious
"images," "pictures," or "stories" which flourish in the creative
imagination of humans and which provide them with a portrait of
the cosmos in which they live. The church in its ministry, as well
as in its theological reflection, must strive both to facilitate
the development of such imagery in the family life and to see that
the warm, loving nature of the husband/wife, parent/child relationships are such that these images can be reinforced and allowed
to flourish.

6) Much of the decline in religious practice among young adults seems
related to alienation and a conflict between sexual permissiveness
and religious norms. But the conflict does not seem to exist
for those with warm images. They are less likely to have permissive

attitudes on sex (and abortion -- though they are politically and socially liberal), and to the extent that they are permissive in their attitudes the impact of this permissiveness on their religious devotion is cancelled out by their religious images. Thus, it would seem that the best way the church can fight both alienation and permissiveness is not by tackling them head on, nor by denouncing them, but by emphasizing the warm "stories of God" it has in its heritage. Young adult work with such emphasis is likely to be more effective than any other apostolic efforts.

7) From the church's point of view the best way to be sure of reclaiming young adults is to see that they marry members of their own faith with whom they can develop shared warm religious images. Unfortunately, we know very little, indeed almost nothing, about the reasons for the choice of a partner who is not Catholic or about the dynamics of husband and wife mutual religious influence in the early years of marriage.

8) The marriage cycle and the religious devotional cycle are intimately related, and the warm images seem to be the phenomenon which link them together. It is not enough for church leaders to say "they'll come back when they get married." Some do and some don't. Whether they do or not is a function mostly of their stories of God, their stories of their marital relationship, and the interaction between the two sets of stories.

9) Warm religious images are the strongest predictors of prayer, hopefulness and social commitment, much stronger than propositional orthodoxy. They are the key factors, it would seem, in personal and familial religious development, but they are totally unaffected by educational attainment, and religious education. Sermons seem

to have an impact on such "stories of God" as does both the family of origin and the family of procreation. We have, in other words, discovered a powerful force in the religious socialization of a human being, but we cannot explain very well the dynamics which might influence the growth of such a force. The Catholic education of our young adults and young families has had no impact whatsoever on the development of their religious imagination (even though it has important effects on other less powerful factors of religious behavior). Thus, it would appear that Catholic schools must pay much greater attention to the image development which occurs in their students. Research and experimentation on how this occurs is extremely important.

10) The development of the religious imagination cannot be isolated from the development of the rest of the human imagination, a development at which modern cognitive education in schools not only does not facilitate, but positively impeeds. We come to school poetic and depart prosaic. American Catholicism must be more deeply concerned about the development of the imagination which seems to be a far more effective dimension of the religious and spiritual life than does propositional catechetics. Without wishing to deny the importance of proposition religion, I think the evidence in this report proves that the raw elemental strength of religion resides in the imaginative dimension of the personality. For much of Catholic history, after all, religion was taught through pictures, images, statues, and stories because there were no schools to pass on elaborate propositional systems. We need the propositional systems today, but we must recapture the educational power of the religious imagination. It would seem that two different kinds of imaginative behavior ought

to be much more strongly reinforced by the church: a) the development of the individual religious imagination through the encouragement of religious "story telling" by young people and b) the reinforcement of the "high imagination" through art, music, poetry and literature. The propensity of many American Catholic leaders, pastoral workers, administrators and teachers to think that the fine and literary arts are at best an unnecessarily expensive luxury would seem foolish to those who built the medieval cathedrals or wrote the medieval religious hymnody. If we told them that we don't need songs, story telling, dances and pictures to pass on religion because we have schools, they might find it hard to understand what we are talking about. The evidence presented in this book suggests that they knew something important which we have forgotten.

11) Whereas we have clearly delineated both the "crisis of passage" through which the young Catholic family goes, its partial origins in families of origin and its intimate relationship to both sexual fulfillment and religious imagery, we have only begun to understand the crisis and the imagery and the issue of sexual fulfillment which is so closely linked with both. Nor do we have any idea what further crises face the Catholic family after the first decade and how sexuality, religious imagery and marital fulfillment will weather these crises. Further research, therefore, would be appropriate both to understand better the dynamics of adjustment, decline and growth in the first decade of the Catholic family's existence, and then to apply this understanding to the problems of subsequent years of marriage and family life. I hope that the findings presented in this report convince the readers how enormously useful social

research might be in the church's ministry. Many religious leaders,
administrators, pastoral workers, and theologians are vaguely aware
that a crisis affects the early years of marriage. The present
research report has provided a detail, a precision and a partial
explanation for the crisis which has hitherto been completely
lacking. It has also provided, if I may say so, astonishing evidence
on how profoundly religious, indeed primordially religious, the crisis
of the first decade of marriage is. I would suspect that many readers
would not have believed before reading this report that there was
really a close link between cosmic religious imagery and sexual
fulfillment. Nor would they have believed that married people have
to strive as long as eight years to pull their relationship out
of the doldrums that begin to set in during the third year of their
relationship. I would like to observe that both of these important
findings were obtained for the church by the minor expense of printing,
mailing and processing 400 questionnaires.

12) I also hope that this report demonstrates to the reader how
extraordinarily useful to the church can be the new theory of religion,
a fragment of which provided the perspective for this report. The
theory is emerging from a convergence of many different disciplines
and can provide extraordinarily rich and useful insights and information
for the church. One need not subscribe to the total truth of the
theory to perceive that it can be extremely useful in generating
information and understanding -- and need not involve theological
controversy which would be embarrassing to church leaders.

13) To summarize in a sentence the theoretical assumption and the
empirical findings of the present report: If you grow up in a warm
family, you are more likely to have "warm" religious imagery; if
you have "warm" religious imagery and grew up in a "warm" family,
you are more likely to have a "warm" sexual life with your spouse;
if you have grown up in a "warm" family, have "warm" religious
imagery, and a "warm" sexual relationship with your spouse, then
you will have a "warm" marriage relationship -- no matter how cold
it may get during the critical years of the middle of the first decade
of your marriage.

14) There is substantial ground for cautious optimism in the present
report. Whereas young Catholics are less devout in their external
religious practice than were their predecessors, they, nonetheless,
maintain strong attachments to the church and to return to religious
devotion as they become reintegrated into society. In particular,
their religious images -- which, perhaps, can be taken as an indirect
measure of their faith -- continue to be strongly and traditionally
Catholic. Furthermore, both their religious imagery and their
religious practice are closely linked to their married love, which
married love in turn seems to facilitate and be facilitated by
frequent prayer. There is little evidence in the data available to
us about this generation that they will drift away from Catholic
loyalties as have their counterparts in many European countries.
On the contrary, I would speculate that by the time they reach the
end of their twenties this generation of young American Catholics
has done all the drifting away from the church they are about to do,
and that neither personality and psychological problems, nor the

behavior of church authority are likely to have much negative impact on their religion. A young Catholic who is in a strong and passionate marriage and whose marriage links him to the church and to the Cosmic Person can not be driven out of the church.

15) There is also grounds for cautious optimism in the rather extraordinary rebound of marital love that occurs at the end of the first decade of marriage. For the most part without help from anyone the young couple is apparently able to pull their marriage together despite the frustrations of the first decade, and grow both in love for one another and together in love for God -- no mean achievement.

16) In the church's ministry both to young adults and to the young family there is much work that has to be done. But, the church does not work completely without certain human dynamics which might assist it. The faith, for instance (as measured by the religious imagination), and the passionate love of young married Catholics are powerful dynamisms which actively and vigorously, if not always self consciously, aid the work of the church. If one wishes to measure the importance of that conclusion as good news, one might imagine what the work of the church might be like if the passionate loves of the young married man and woman for each other were working against the mission of the church.

APPENDIX A

23. When you think about God, how likely are each of these images to come to your mind?

(CIRCLE ONE NUMBER FOR EACH WORD)

	Extremely likely	Somewhat likely	Not too likely	Not likely at all
Judge	1	2	3	4
Protector	1	2	3	4
Redeemer	1	2	3	4
Lover	1	2	3	4
Master	1	2	3	4
Mother	1	2	3	4
Creator	1	2	3	4
Father	1	2	3	4

24. Here are some words people sometimes associate with Jesus. How likely is each one of them to come to your mind when you think about Jesus?

(CIRCLE ONE NUMBER FOR EACH WORD)

	Extremely likely	Somewhat likely	Not too likely	Not likely at all
Gentle	1	2	3	4
Stern	1	2	3	4
Warm	1	2	3	4
Distant	1	2	3	4
Demanding	1	2	3	4
Patient	1	2	3	4
Irrelevant	1	2	3	4
Challenging	1	2	3	4
Comforting	1	2	3	4

25. Now think about Jesus' mother, Mary. How likely is each word to come to your mind when you think of Mary?

(CIRCLE ONE NUMBER FOR EACH WORD)

	Extremely likely	Somewhat likely	Not too likely	Not likely at all
Gentle	1	2	3	4
Stern	1	2	3	4
Warm	1	2	3	4
Distant	1	2	3	4
Demanding	1	2	3	4
Patient	1	2	3	4
Irrelevant	1	2	3	4
Challenging	1	2	3	4
Comforting	1	2	3	4

APPENDIX A (cont.)

31. Here is a situation in which some people actually find themselves. Imagine that this is happening to you. How close would each of the following statements be to your own reaction to such a situation?

   You have just visited your doctor and he has told you that you have less than a year to live. He has said that your disease is incurable.

   PLEASE CIRCLE A NUMBER ON EACH LINE TO INDICATE IF THE STATEMENT COMES VERY CLOSE TO YOUR FEELINGS, NOT AT ALL CLOSE TO YOUR FEELINGS OR IS SOMEWHERE IN BETWEEN THESE FEELINGS.

	Very close .... Not at all close
A. It will all work out for the best somehow	1 ... 2 ... 3 ... 4 ... 5
B. No one should question the goodness of God's decision about death	1 ... 2 ... 3 ... 4 ... 5
C. There is nothing to do but wait for the end	1 ... 2 ... 3 ... 4 ... 5
D. I am angry and depressed at the unfairness of it all	1 ... 2 ... 3 ... 4 ... 5
E. I am thankful for the life that I have had	1 ... 2 ... 3 ... 4 ... 5
F. I cannot explain why this has happened to me, but I still believe in God's love	1 ... 2 ... 3 ... 4 ... 5

APPENDIX A (cont.)

32. Here is another situation in which some people actually find themselves. Imagine that one of your parents is dying a slow and painful death. How close would each of the following statements be to your own reaction to such a situation?

PLEASE CIRCLE A NUMBER ON EACH LINE TO INDICATE IF THE STATEMENT COMES VERY CLOSE TO YOUR FEELINGS, NOT AT ALL CLOSE TO YOUR FEELINGS OR IS SOMEWHERE IN BETWEEN THESE FEELINGS.

	Very close .... Not at all close
A. They are in pain now, but they will be at peace soon	1 ... 2 ... 3 ... 4 ... 5
B. Everything that happens is God's will and cannot be bad	1 ... 2 ... 3 ....4 ... 5
C. There is nothing to do but wait for the end	1 ... 2 ... 3 ... 4 ... 5
D. This waiting is inhuman for them; I hope it will end soon	1 ... 2 ... 3 ... 4 ... 5
E. We can at least be thankful for the good life we have had together	1 ... 2 ... 3 ... 4 ... 5
F. This is tragic, but death is not the ultimate end for us	1 ... 2 ... 3 ... 4 ... 5

33. Do you believe there is life after death?

(CIRCLE ONE)

Yes .... 1 - *ANSWER A*
No .... 2 - *GO TO 34*
Don't know ....8 - *ANSWER A*

A.   Of course, no one knows exactly what life after death would be like, but here are some ideas people have had.

How likely do you feel each possibility is?

(CIRCLE ONE NUMBER BESIDE EACH IDEA)

	Very likely	Somewhat likely	Not too likely	Not likely at all
1. A life of peace and tranquility	1	2	3	4
2. A life of intense action	1	2	3	4
3. A life like the one here on earth only better	1	2	3	4
4. A life without many things which make our present life enjoyable	1	2	3	4
5. A pale shadowy form of life, hardly life at all	1	2	3	4
6. A spiritual life, involving our mind but not our body	1	2	3	4
7. A paradise of pleasure and delights	1	2	3	4
8. A place of loving intellectual communion	1	2	3	4
9. Union with God	1	2	3	4
10. Reunion with loved ones	1	2	3	4

118. Taking all things into consideration, how satisfied are you with your marriage these days? Would you say you are very satisfied, moderately satisfied, or not satisfied at all?

(CIRCLE ONE)

Very satisfied 1

Moderately satisfied 2

Not satisfied at all ... 3

126. How would you rate your marriage on the following aspects of your relationship?

(CIRCLE ONE NUMBER FOR EACH PHRASE)

		Excellent	Very good	Good	Fair	Poor
A.	Ability to talk about problems with my spouse.	1	2	3	4	5
B.	Emotional satisfaction.	1	2	3	4	5
C.	Confidence in the stability of our marriage.	1	2	3	4	5
D.	Agreement on financial issues.	1	2	3	4	5
E.	Opportunity to express love and affection.	1	2	3	4	5
F.	Sexual fulfillment.	1	2	3	4	5
G.	Agreement on basic values.	1	2	3	4	5
H.	Ability to express disagreement without threatening the relationship.	1	2	3	4	5
I.	Agreement on religious issues.	1	2	3	4	5

ANSWER THE NEXT QUESTION ONLY IF YOU HAVE CHILDREN

J.	Agreement on how to raise children.	1	2	3	4	5

TABLE 1.1

RELIGIOUS INTERMARRIAGE AMONG YOUNG CATHOLICS

Spouses Religion	Percent
Catholic	54.0
Jewish	1.0
Baptist	5.0
Methodist	7.0
Presbyterians	4.0
Lutheran	5.0
Episcopal	2.0
Other	9.0
None	13.0

TABLE 1.2

VALID MARRIAGES FOR YOUNG CATHOLICS

Variable	Percent
Married by priest	66.0
Not married by priest	34.0

TABLE 1.3

MARITAL STATUS OF "NOT SINGLE" YOUNG CATHOLICS

Marital Status	Percent
Married	81.0
Widowed	1.0
Divorced	6.0
Separated	4.0
Living together	8.0
Total	100.0

TABLE 1.4

MARITAL SATISFACTION FOR YOUNG CATHOLICS

Marital Satisfaction	Percent
Very satisfied	67.0
Moderately satisfied	30.0
Not satisfied at all	3.0

TABLE 1.5

MARRIAGE "RELATIONSHIP RATINGS" FOR YOUNG CATHOLICS

	Excellent	Very Good	Good	Fair	Poor
Ability to discuss problems with spouse .	35.4	34.5	14.3	11.9	4.0
Emotional satisfaction in marriage	33.4	35.9	18.8	8.8	3.0
Confidence in stability of marriage	48.5	27.7	14.6	5.8	3.4
Financial agreement in marriage	32.0	36.6	18.6	7.9	4.9
Express affection in marriage	44.5	29.9	18.3	5.5	1.8
Sexual fulfillment in marriage	43.9	23.8	19.2	9.5	3.7
Basic values agree in marriage	38.2	31.2	23.9	5.8	.9
Disagree okay marriage	34.1	29.9	19.2	11.9	4.9
Religious agreement in marriage	19.2	29.0	25.3	17.1	9.5
Child techniques agree in R marriage	33.3	37.3	20.4	8.5	.5

TABLE 1.6

MARITAL SATISFACTION FOR YOUNG CATHOLICS
BY CERTAIN BACKGROUND VARIABLES

Variable	Percent very satisfied
Sex:	
Men	75.0[a]
Women	61.0
Children present:	
Yes	67.0
No	66.0
Education:	
College graduate	74.0
Not college graduate . . .	64.0
Race:	
White	69.0[a]
Not white	54.0
Working wife:	
Yes	68.0
No	61.0
Raised by both parents:	
Yes	66.0
No	66.0
Divorced:	
Yes	57.0
No	68.0[a]
Mixed marriage:	
Yes	63.0
No	71.0[a]
Married by priest:	
Yes	70.0
No	60.0[a]

[a]Difference statistically significant.

TABLE 1.7

MARRIAGE RELATIONSHIP RATINGS FOR YOUNG CATHOLICS
BY CERTAIN BACKGROUND VARIABLES

(Percent Excellent)

	Sexual fulfillment	Emotional satisfaction	Basic value agreement
Sex:			
Men	42	34	35
Women	45	33	40
Children present:			
Yes	40*	29*	37
No	49*	39*	40
Education:			
College graduate	38	39	40
Not college graduate . .	46	31	38
Race:			
White	44	35*	40*
Not white	47	20	29
Working wife:			
Yes	48	35	37
No	43	24	34
Raised by both parents:			
Yes	44	33	39
No	46	33	38
Divorced:			
Yes	40	27	30
No	44	34	39
Mixed marriage:			
Yes	46	34	39
No , ...	46	33	37
Married by priest:			
Yes	44	32	39
No	45	37	37

*Difference statistically significant

TABLE 1.8

MARITAL SATISFACTION AND DURATION OF MARRIAGE

Duration	Percent very satisfied
Less than 2 years	76(72)
3-4 years	66(64)
5-6 years	64(66)
7-8 years	57(43)
9-10 years.	79(43)

TABLE 1.9

MARITAL SATISFACTION AND DURATION OF MARRIAGE BY SEX

Duration	Percent very satisfied	
	Men	Women
Less than 2 years	71	82
3-4 years	72	57
5-6 years	82	55
7-8 years	77	46
9-10 years	87	75

TABLE 1.10

RATING OF MARRIAGE RELATIONSHIPS

	Percent excellent		
	Sexual fulfillment	Emotional satisfaction	Value consensus
Less than two years	57	49	49
3-4 years	34	27	32
5-6 years	36	33	33
7-8 years	42	26	39
9-10 years	54	33	44

TABLE 1.11

MARRIAGE RATINGS BY NUMBER OF CHILDREN

Number of children	Percent excellent	
	Sexual fulfillment	Emotional satisfaction
0 . . .	49	39
1 . . .	32	26
2+ . . .	49	34

TABLE 1.12

SEXUAL FULFILLMENT, NUMBER OF CHILDREN
AND LENGTH OF MARRIAGE

(Percent excellent)

Duration of marriage	Number of children		
	0	1	2+
0-2	56(54)	57(14)	a
3-4	36(40)	29(21)	a
5-6	52(21)	12(26)	53(19)
7-8	50(12)	32(22)	47(30)
9-10	a	60(10)	52(29)

[a] Less than 5 cases.

TABLE 1.13

A WOMAN'S MARITAL SATISFACTION BY HER HUSBAND'S
RATING OF THE SEXUAL FULFILLMENT
IN THEIR RELATIONSHIP

Rating	Percent very satisfied
Women:	
Husband reporting sexual fulfillment "excellent"	79 (67)
"Not excellent"	52 (119)
Men:	
Wife reporting sexual fulfillment "excellent"	73 (48)
"Not excellent"	76 (82)

TABLE 1.14

HUSBAND'S RATING OF SEXUAL FULFILLMENT
IN MARRIAGE BY LENGTH OF MARRIAGE

Length of marriage	Percent excellent
Less than 2 years	45
3-4 years	33
5-6 years	34
7-8 years	20
9-10 years	46

TABLE 1.15

MARITAL SATISFACTION FOR WOMEN BY SPOUSE'S
RATING OF SEXUAL FULFILLMENT IN MARRIAGE
AS EXCELLENT BY DURATION OF MARRIAGE

(Percent very satisfied)

Duration of marriage	Spouse rates sexual fulfillment as excellent	Does not
0-2 years	94 (17)	71 (21)
3-8 years	65 (32)	48 (77)
9-10 years	92 (13)	60 (15)

TABLE 1.16

MARITAL SATISFACTION BY DURATION OF MARRIAGE BY MIXED MARRIAGE

(Percent very satisfied)

Duration of marriage	Catholic marriage	Mixed marriage
Less than 2 years . . .	77(34)	76(38)
3-4 years	68(35)	62(29)
5-6 years	71(34)	55(31)
7-8 years	62(34)	58(29)
9-10 years	89(26)	69(17)

TABLE 1.17

MARITAL SATISFACTION AND "LIVING TOGETHER"

	Married	"Living together"
Percent very satisfied .	67(375)	50*(31)

*Statistically significant

TABLE 1.18

RATING RELATIONSHIP AS "STABLE" AND "LIVING TOGETHER"

	Married	"Living together"
Percent "excellent" stability	49	20*

*Statistically significant

TABLE 1.19

MARITAL SATISFACTION, MARITAL STABILITY
"EXCELLENT" AND LIVING TOGETHER

(Percent very satisfied

	Stability "excellent"	Not "excellent"
Married	90** (182)	45** (190
Living together	100 (6)	36 (22)

**N.S.

TABLE 1.20

MARITAL SATISFACTION, AND LIVING TOGETHER BY SEX

	Men		Women	
	Married	Living together	Married	Living together
Percent very satisfied .	74	33*	62	54**

*Statistically significant

**N.S.

TABLE 2.1

JOINT SATISFACTION BY LENGTH OF MARRIAGE

Length of marriage	Percent both "very satisfied"
0 -2 years	65
3-8 years	50^{*}
9-10 years	70^{**}

*Decline statistically significant

**Increase statistically significant

TABLE 2.2

MARITAL SATISFACTION BY COHORT BY DURATION OF MARRIAGE

(Percent both "very satisfied")

Duration of Marriage	25-27 Years old	28-30 Years old
0-2 years	57 (14)	36 (8)
3-8 years	56 (71)	50 (80)
9-10 years	64 (11)	72 (32)

TABLE 2.3

CORRELATIONS BETWEEN SPOUSES ON MARRIAGE RATINGS

Ability to talk with spouse 46

Emotional satisfaction 52

Confidence in stability 55

Financial agreement 41

Opportunity to express love and affection . . .44

Sexual fulfillment 42

Value agreement 42

Ability to express disagreement 38

Religious agreement 49

Agreement on how to raise children 49

TABLE 2.4

RAW CORRELATIONS BETWEEN JOINT SATISFACTION
(BOTH "VERY SATISFIED") AND AGREEMENT
ON MARRIAGE RATINGS (BOTH "EXCELLENT")

Joint satisfaction

Agreement as "excellent"

Talk	.39
Emotions	.38
Finances	.20
Love and affection	.30
Sexual fulfillment	.32
Values	
Disagreement (expression of)	.32
Religious agreement	.15

NOTE: All relationships are statistically significant

TABLE 2.6

JOINT SATISFACTION BY AGREEMENT ON SEXUAL FULFILLMENT
BY DURATION OF MARRIAGE

(Percent both "very satisfied")

Duration of marriage	Fulfillmentnnot "excellent"	"Excellent"
0-2 years	58	86
3-8 years	45	78 *
9-10 years	50	100 **

*Statistically significant

**N.S.

TABLE 2.7

JOINT SATISFACTION BY AGREEMENT ON VALUE CONCENSUS
BY DURATION OF MARRIAGE

(Percent both "very satisfied")

Duration of marriage	Fulfillment not "excellent"	"Excellent"
0-2 years	58	84
3-8 years	45	73
9-10 years.	55	100

TABLE 2.8

CORRELATIONS BETWEEN JOINT MARITAL SATISFACTION,
SEXUAL FULFILLMENT (BOTH "EXCELLENT")
AND ATTITUDES ON LIVING TOGETHER

	Sexual fulfillment	Marital satisfaction
Birth control . . .	.05	.01
Divorce	.02	.04
Premarital sex . .	.00	.04
Living together . .	.03	.03

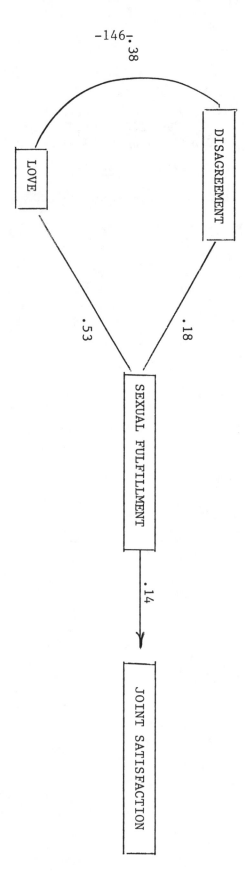

TABLE 2.9

RELATIONSHIP AMONG "LOVE AND AFFECTION," ABILITY TO "EXPRESS DISAGREEMENT,"
"SEXUAL FULFILLMENT" AND JOINT SATISFACTION

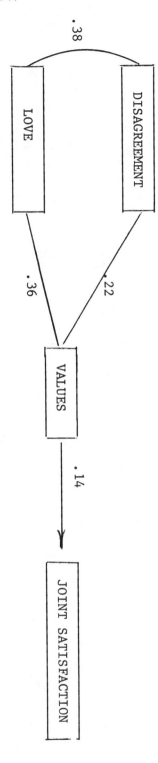

TABLE 2.10

RELATIONSHIP AMONG "LOVE AND AFFECTION," ABILITY TO
"EXPRESS DISAGREEMENT," VALUE CONSENSUS
AND JOINT SATISFACTION

TABLE 3.1

JOINT SATISFACTION AND RATING AGREEMENT BY CERTAIN RELIGIOUS MEASURES

	Joint marital satisfaction (both "very satisfied")	Sexual fulfillment (both "excellent")	Value consensus (both "excellent")
Frequent prayer	.12*	.10*	.17*
Frequent church	.09*	.12*	.06
Belief in after life . .	.16*	.13*	.11*
Married by priest . . .	.09*	.08*	.04
Mixed marriage	.00	.06	-.08*
Divorce	-.09*	.05	.06

TABLE 3.2

CHURCH ATTENDANCE AND MARITAL SATISFACTION RATINGS

	Both frequent attendance	Both not frequent attendance
Marital satisfaction (Percent both very satisfied)	64*	51
Sexual fulfillment (Percent both excellent) . .	37*	25
Value concensus (Percent both excellent) . .	29*	19

*Statistically significant

TABLE 3.3

PRAYER AND MARITAL SATISFACTION

	Both frequent prayer	Not both frequent prayer
Marital satisfaction . .	63*	52
Sexual fulfillment . . .	31	26
Value consensus	28*	19

*Statistically significant

TABLE 3.4

AFTER LIFE BELIEF AND MARITAL SATISFACTION

	Both believe in life after death	Not both believe in life after death
Marital satisfaction . .	64*	49
Sexual fulfillment . . .	34*	22
Value consensus	27*	16

*Statistically significant

TABLE 3.5

MARITAL STATUS AND MARITAL SATISFACTION

	Marital satisfaction (both very satisfied)
Married by priest	58[*]
Not married by priest	49
Not divorced	57[*]
Divorced	41

TABLE 3.6A

MARITAL SATISFACTION IN MIXED MARRIGES BY DURATION

(Percent both very satisfied)

	Catholic marriage	Mixed marriage
0-2 years	65	65
3-8 years	52[*]	48[*]
9-10 years	70[**]	59

[*]Decline statistically significant

[**] Rise statistically significant

TABLE 3.6B

RELIGIOUS DEVOTION SCALE BY DURATION OF MARRIAGE

0-2 years	59
3-8 years	44[*]
9-10 years	58[**]

[*]Decline statistically significant

[**]Rise statistically significant

TABLE 3.7

MARITAL SATISFACTION BY RELIGIOUS DEVOTION BY DURATION OF MARRIAGE

(Percent both "very satisfied")

	Religious devotion	
	Low	High
0-2 years	69 (42)	67 (22)
3-8 years	44* (133)	62 (53)
9-10 years	58** (24)	82** (17)

*

TABLE 3.8

MARRIAGE RATINGS BY RELIGION SCALE BY LENGTH OF MARRIAGE

(Percent both "excellent")

	Sexual fulfillment		Value consensus	
	Religion scale		Religion scale	
	High	Low	High	Low
0-2 years	38	33	30	33
3-8 years	23[*]	21[*]	22[*]	21[*]
9-10 years	53[**]	33	41[**]	25

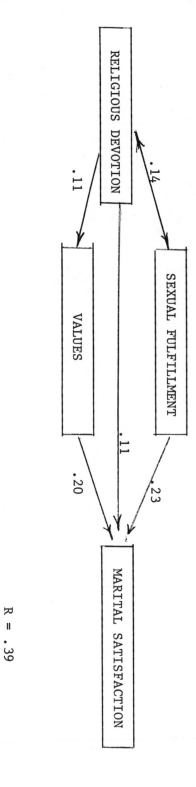

TABLE 3.9

R = .39

TABLE 4.1

RELIGIOUS IMAGERY AMONG YOUNG CATHOLICS

	United States	Canada	(French Canadians)
Images of Jesus (percent "Extremely likely")			
Gentle	70	72	
Stern	18	11	
Warm	68	62	
Distant	11	17	(20)
Demanding	10	15	
Patient	71	69	
Irrelevant	3	7	
Challenging	20	18	
Comforting	69	65	
Images of Mary			
Gentle	84	85	
Stern	7	4	
Warm	78	70	(67)
Distant	9	24	(34)
Demanding	4	6	
Patient	73	70	
Irrelevant	4	6	
Challenging	7	7	
Comforting	75	69	
Images of God			
Judge	28	19	
Protector	57	54	
Redeemer	45	38	
Lover	30	60	(70)
Master	44	38	
Mother	12	17	(21)
Creator	74	73	
Father	62	62	
Images of Heaven			
A life of peace and tranquility	52	47	

RELIGIOUS IMAGERY AMONG YOUNG CATHOLICS
(continued)

A life of intense action	4	5
A life like the one here on earth only better	21	18
A life without many things which make our present life enjoyable	14	11
A pale shadowy form of life, hardly life at all	2	3
A spiritual life, involving our mind but not our body	36	41
A paradise of pleasure and delights	20	24
A place of loving intellectual communion	35	30
Union with God	64	54
Reunion with loved ones	56	49

TABLE 4.1B

SEXUAL FULFILLMENT IN MARRIAGE AND VALUE CONSENSUS BY WARM IMAGE
SCALE
(percent "Excellent")

Image Scale	Sexual fulfillment	Value consensus
0 (low)	33 (75)	27
1	38 (97)	25
2	48 (121)	47
3	53 (80)	48
4 (high)	69 (16)	63

TABLE 4.2

JOINT RELIGIOUS IMAGERY (HUSBAND AND
WIFE BOTH)

Religious Imagery	Percent
God as "lover"	12
Jesus as "warm"	51
Mary as "warm"	53
Afterlife a paradise of pleasure and delight . . .	5

TABLE 4.3

CORRELATIONS BETWEEN SPOUSES'
RELIGIOUS IMAGERY

Religious Imagery

God as "lover" 24*

Jesus as "warm" 10*

Mary as "warm" 08*

Afterlife a paradise of
   pleasure and delight . . .24*

TABLE 4.4

CORRELATION BETWEEN JOINT IMAGE SCALE
AND MARITAL ADJUSTMENTS

Marital satisfaction 12*

Sexual fulfillment 21*

Value consensus 18*

TABLE 4.5

JOINT MARITAL ADJUSTMENT BY JOINT IMAGE SCALE

Marital Adjustment	Image Scale	
	High ("Warm")	Low ("Cool")
Percent both "very satisfied"	69*	53
Percent both "excellent" sexual adjustment	36*	22
Percent both "excellent" value consensus	30	18

TABLE 4.6

IMAGE SCALE BY DURATION OF MARRIAGE

(Z-scores)

Duration of Marriage	Z-score
0-2 years	.25
3-8 years	-.13
9-10 years	.23**

TABLE 4.7

CORRELATIONS BETWEEN SPOUSE'S IMAGE OF GOD AS LOVER AND
HEAVEN AS PARADISE OF DELIGHT AT BEGINNING OF
MARRIAGE AND AFTER A DECADE

Years of Marriage	God	Afterlife
0-2 years	.05	-.14
8-10 years	.40*	.23*

TABLE 4.8

GOD AS LOVER BY SPOUSE'S IMAGE OF GOD AS LOVER BY
DURATION OF MARRIAGE

(Percent "Extremely likely")

Duration of Marriage	Spouse	
	"Extremely likely"	Not
0-2 Years	79	50
3-8 Years	51*	27*
9-10 Years	67**	12*

TABLE 4.8B

IMAGE OF GOD AS LOVER BY SPOUSE'S IMAGE BY SATISFACTION
OF BOTH WITH SEXUAL FULFILLMENT

(Percent Responded God as Lover)

Image	Both "Excellent"	Not
Spouse "extremely likely" to imagine God as lover	71*	56*
Not	24	31

TABLE 4.9

IMAGE OF GOD AS MOTHER

Image	Percent
Extremely likely . . .	7
Somewhat likely . . .	12
Not too likely . . .	27
Not likely at all . .	54
Total	100

TABLE 4.10

GOD AS MOTHER BY SPOUSE'S IMAGE OF
GOD AS MOTHER

(Percent Extremely or Somewhat Likely)

Spouse extremely or somewhat likely . . . 28

Spouse not 17

TABLE 4.11

ASSOCIATION BETWEEN IMAGE OF GOD AS MOTHER BETWEEN
SPOUSES FOR LENGTH OF MARRIAGE

Years of Marriage		Gamma
0-3 Years	. . . .	.27
5-6 Years	. . . .	.57
7-8 Years	. . . .	.58

TABLE 4.12

IMAGE OF GOD AS MOTHER BY SPOUSE'S IMAGE BY
MARITAL SATISFACTION

Marital Satisfaction	Gamma
Very satisfied	.37
Not satisfied	.16

TABLE 4.13

CORRELATIONS BETWEEN FAMILY EXPERIENCES GROWING UP AND
JOINT MARITAL SATISFACTION AND JOINT
RELATIONSHIP RATINGS

| | "Happy" as Child | Respondent Close to: | |
		Father	Mother
Joint satisfaction	.17*	.04	.10*
Joint "excellent"			
Sexual fulfillment	.10*	.09*	.05
Value consensus	.09*	.05	.17*

TABLE 4.14

MODEL TO EXPLAIN DECLINEOOF SEXUAL FULFILLMENT (BOTH SPOUSES
"EXCELLENT") BETWEEN THE FIRST TWO YEARS OF MARRIAGE AND
THIRD TO EIGHTH YEARS OF MARRIAGE

	Difference	Proportion of Decline Explained
Simple difference	-13%	
Taking into account closeness to mother, spouse's closeness to mother, and happiness of childhood	-10%	.23
+		
"Warm" religious imagery	-7%	.46
+		
Ability to express love and affection	-5%	.62

TABLE 4.15

MODEL TO EXPLAIN INCREASE OF SEXUAL FULFILLMENT (BOTH
SPOUSES "EXCELLENT") BETWEEN THE THIRD AND EIGHTH
YEARS OF MARRIAGE AND THE NINTH AND TENTH YEARS

	Difference	Proportion of Increase Explained
Simple difference	+21%	
Taking into account closeness to mother, spouse's closeness to mother, and happiness of childhood	+19%	.18
+		
"Warm" religious imagery	+8%	.62
+		
Ability to express love and affection	+6%	.75

TABLE 4.16

MODEL TO EXPLAIN DECLINE OF MARITAL SATISFACTION (BOTH
"VERY SATISFIED") FROM FIRST TO SECOND YEARS OF
MARRIAGE TO THIRD TO EIGHTH YEARS

	Difference	Proportion of Decline Explained
Simple difference	-19%	
Taking into account closeness to mother, spouse's closeness to mother, and happiness of childhood	-17%	.11
+		
"Warm" religious imagery	-8%	.58
+		
Ability to express love and affection	-5%	.68
+		
Sexual fulfillment	-5%	.68

TABLE 4.17

MODEL TO EXPLAIN INCREASE OF MARITAL SATISFACTION FROM
THIRD TO EIGHTH YEARS OF MARRIAGE TO NINTH TO
TENTH YEARS OF MARRIAGE

	Difference	Proportion of Increase Explained
Simple difference	+20%	
Taking into account closeness to mother, spouse's closeness to mother, and happiness of childhood	+19%	.05
+		
"Warm" religious imagery	+16%	.20
+		
Ability to express love and affection	+12%	.40
+		
Sexual fulfillment	+9%	.55

TABLE 4.18

DATA TO TEST MODEL PROPOSED IN FIGURE 4.2

A. Sexual Fulfillment by Religious Experience
(Percent "Excellent")

Religious experience often or sometimes	64*
Rarely or never	43

B. God as Lover by Religious Experience
(Percent "Extremely Likely")

Religious experience often or sometimes	59*
Rarely or never	39

C. Sexual Fulfillment by Religious Experience by
Image of God as Lover
(Percent "Excellent")

	God as Lover Extremely Likely	Not
Religious experience often or sometimes	69*	48
Rarely or never	50	40

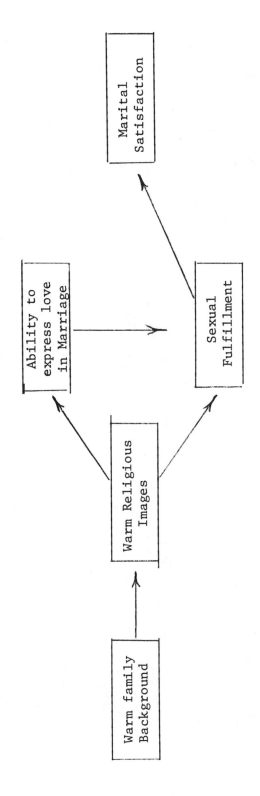

Fig. 4.1. Model demonstrating the hypothesized relationships in this chapter

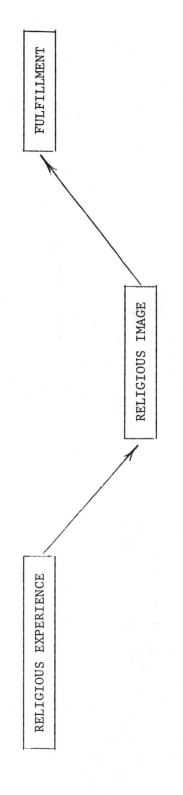

Fig. 4.2. Hypothesized model for relationship among religious experience, image of God as lover and sexual fulfillment in marriage

-179-

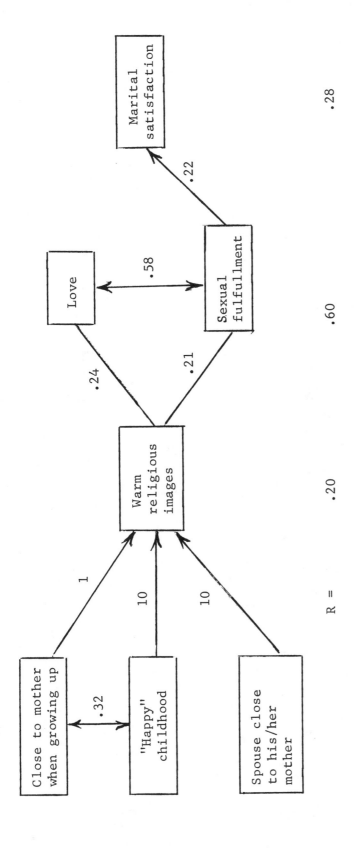

Fig. 4.3. Test of basic model for sexual fulfillment (both spouses "excellent") and marital satisfaction (both spouses "very satisfied")

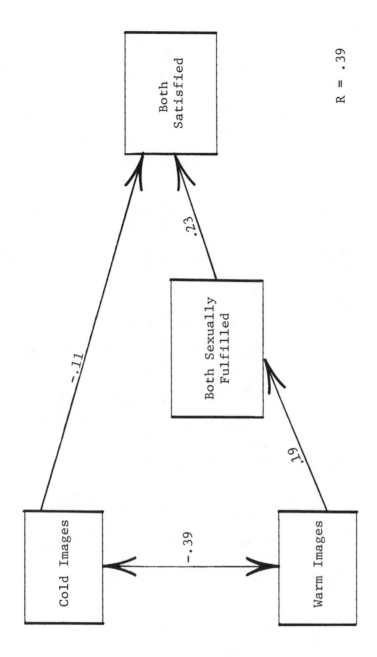

Figure 4A.1. Model for cold images and marital adjustment

TABLE 5.1

RELIGIOUS PRACTICE BY COHORT BY COUNTRY

(Percent high on devotion scale)[1]

	USA	Canada
14-17 years old . .	64	53
18-21 years old . .	48	40
22-25 years old . .	33	21
26-28 years old . .	22*	19*
29-30 years old . .	29**	25**
Average	39***	31

[1]Scale composed of prayer, mass attendance and reception of communion. To be high on the scale the respondent has to do two of the three following: pray every day or at least several times a week, go to mass every week, receive communion several times a month.

*In both the USA and Canada the decline in devotion is statistically significant.

**When Canada and the United States are combined the rise at the end of the 20's is statistically significant.

***The average devotional level for the United States is higher than that for Canada at a statistically significant level.

TABLE 5.2

RELIGIOUS LIFE CYCLE BY SEX

(Percent High on Devotion Scale)

	USA	Canada
	Male	
14-17 years old . .	60.2 (118)	48.3 (58)
18-21 years old . .	41.4 (157)	39.5 (81)
22-25 years old . .	24.8 (149)	15.5 (84)
26-28 years old . .	17.7 (158) *	13.5 (74)
29-30 years old . .	22.4 (67) **	13.8 (29)
Average . . .	33.3 (649)	26.7 (326)
	Female	
14-17 years old . .	68.7 (115)	59.5 (84)
18-21 years old . .	53.0 (181)	41.1 (107)
22-25 years old . .	42.8 (145)	25.5 (106)
26-28 years old . .	27.2 (184) *	23.3 (86)
29-30 years old . .	33.7 (89)	34.2 (38)
Average . . .	44.4 (714)	36.6 (421)

*In both the USA and Canada the decline in devotion is statistically significant.

**When Canada and the United States are combined the rise at the end of the 20's is statistically significant.

TABLE 5.3

RELIGIOUS LIFE CYCLE IN CANADA BY LANGUAGE GROUP

(Percent high on devotional index)

	English	French
14-17 years old . .	55.0 (40)	52.8 (106)
18-21 years old . .	37.5 (72)	41.5 (118)
22-25 years old . .	27.7 (65)	18.0 (128)
26-28 years old . .	16.3 (43)	18.8 (117)*
29-30 years old . .	31.8 (22)	22.7 (44)**
Average . . .	33.5 (242)	31.2 (513)

*In both the USA and Canada the decline in devotion is statistically significant.

**When Canada and the United States are combined the rise at the end of the 20's is statistically significant.

TABLE 5.4

RELIGIOUS LIFE CYCLE IN CANADA BY MOTHER TONGUE BY SEX

	English	French
	Male	
14-17 years old . .	60.0 (20)	42.1 (38)
18-21 years old . .	30.0 (30)	45.1 (51)
22-25 years old . .	17.2 (29)	14.5 (55)
26-28 years old . .	9.1 (22)	13.7 (51)
29-30 years old . .	20.0 (10)	11.1 (18)
	27.0 (111)	26.3 (213)
	Female	
14-17 years old . .	55.6 (18)	60.6 (66)
18-21 years old . .	42.9 (42)	40.6 (64)
22-25 years old . .	37.1 (35)	19.7 (71)
26-28 years old . .	23.8 (21)	23.4 (64)
29-30 years old . .	41.7 (12)	30.8 (26)
	39.8 (128)	35.4 (291)

TABLE 5.5

PERMISSIVENESS, ALIENATION FROM THE CHURCH AND ORGANIZATIONAL
ALIENATION IN THE UNITED STATES AND CANADA

Mean scores (Standard deviations)

	Permissiveness	Alien from church	Organizational alienation
USA . . .	6.5(1.9)	3.5(1.1)	8.0(2.2)
Canada . .	7.1(1.5)	3.2(1.2)	14.4(2.5)

TABLE 5.6

SEXUAL ATTITUDES IN THE UNITED STATES AND CANADA

	USA	Canada
Living together not wrong . .	51	71
Premarital sex not wrong . . .	54	74

TABLE 5.7

SEXUAL PERMISSIVENESS BY COHORT BY NATION

(z scores)

	USA	Canada
18-21 years old . .	-.21	-.26
22-25 years old . .	.13	.10
26-28 years old . .	.06	.06
29-30 years old . .	-.13	.07

TABLE 5.8

ALIENATION FROM THE CHURCH BY COHORT BY NATION

(z scores)

	USA	Canada
14-17 years old . .	-.36	-.41
18-21 years old . .	-.20	-.04
22-25 years old . .	+.09	+.08
26-28 years old . .	+.29	+.30
29-30 years old . .	+.19	+.05

TABLE 5.9

ORGANIZATIONAL ALIENATION BY COHORT BY COUNTRY

(z scores)

	USA	Canada
18-21 years old . .	-.33	-.10
22-25 years old . .	+.02	-.04
26-28 years old . .	+.12	.12
29-30 years old . .	+.08	-.05

TABLE 5.10

CORRELATES WITH RELIGIOUS DEVOTION BY COUNTRY

(r)

	USA	Canada
Married	.20	.12
Spouse Catholic . .	.12	.03
Organizational alienation . . .	-.13	-.13
Sexual permissiveness .	-.27	-.45
Alienation from the church . . .	-.38	-.45

NOTE: All correlations significant except the second one in the Canadian column.

TABLE 5.11

CORRELATES WITH RELIGIOUS DEVOTION FOR
NON-MARRIED RESPONDENTS BY COUNTRY

	USA	Canada
Organizational alienation . . .	-.18	-.15
Sexual permissiveness	-.34	-.39
Closeness to church	-.40	-.42

TABLE 5.12

RELIGIOUS DEVOTION BY COHORT BY COUNTRY
FOR NON-MARRIEDS

(Percent high on devotion scale)

	USA	Canada
18-21 years old . .	48	32
22-25 years old . .	30	21
26-28 years old . .	19	15
29-30 years old . .	18	16

TABLE 5.13

MODEL TO EXPLAIN DECLINE IN RELIGIOUS DEVOTION
AMONG YOUNG PEOPLE IN TEH UNITED STATES AND
CANADA BETWEEN 18-21 YEAR AND 26-28 YEAR

	USA		Canada	
	Difference	Proportion explained	Difference	Proportion explained
Decline	-26%		-21%	
Taking into account marriage and religiousness of spouse . .	-03%	.88	- 7%	.66

TABLE 5.14

MODEL TO EXPLAIN RISE IN RELIGIOUS DEVOTION BETWEEN
26-28 YEAR AND 29-30 YEAR

	USA		Canada	
	Difference	Proportion explained	Difference	Proportion explained
Increase	+ 7%		+ 6%	
Taking into account marriage and religiousness of spouse . .	+ 1%	.86	+ 3%	.50

TABLE 5.15

MODEL TO EXPLAIN DECLINE IN RELIGIOUS DEVOTION
AMONG NON-MARRIED IN UNITED STATES AND CANADA

	USA		Canada	
	Difference	Proportion explained	Difference	Proportion explained
Decline	−30%		−16%	
Organizational alienation	−23%	.23	−13%	.19
Sexual permissiveness . . .	−18%	.40	− 4%	.75
Alienation from the church . . .	−12%	.60	0%	1.00

TABLE 5.16

MARITAL STATUS OF AMERICAN CATHOLICS BY COHORT

Cohort	Single-not married	Mixed marriage	Catholic marriage	Total
18-21 years	91	6	3	100
22-25 years	69	14	17	100
26-28 years	44	28	28	100
29-30 years	28	26	46	100

TABLE 5.17

RELIGIOUS DEVOTION BY MARITAL STATUS BY COHORT

(Percent high on devotion scale)

	USA			Canada		
	Not married	Mixed marriage	Catholic marriage	Not married	Mixed marriage	Catholic marriage
18-21 years old	48	20	43	32	*	*
22-25 years old	29	33	51	21	23	17
26-28 years old	19	16	35	15	*	21
29-30 years old	18	20	46	23	*	31

*Less than ten cases (only 27 out of 206 Canadian marriages are not with other Catholics).

TABLE 5.18

RELIGIOUS DEVOTION BY MARITAL STATUS

(Percent high on religious devotion scale)

Cohort	Mixed marriage	Catholic marriage	
		Spouse low on religious devotion scale	Spouse high on religious devotion scale
22-25 years old .	14	27	81*
26-28 years old .	28	12	67*
29-30 years old .	26	13	72*

*Significantly different from spouse-with-low-devotion respondents.

TABLE 5.19

MODEL TO EXPLAIN DIFFERENCE IN RELIGIOUS DEVOTION
IN CATHOLIC MARRIAGES BETWEEN THOSE WHO HAVE
DEVOUT SPOUSES AND THOSE WHO DON'T

	Difference	Proportion explained
Increase	+55%	
Family background taken into account	+55%	.00
Warm religious images . . .	+40%	.27
Alienation from Church . .	+28%	.45

TABLE 5.20

DIFFERENCES BETWEEN THOSE WITH HIGH AND LOW RELIGIOUSLY
DEVOUT SPOUSES USING EXPLANATORY MODEL IN TABLE 5.19

	Without model	With model
22–25 years old	54%	28%
26–28 years old	55	27
29–30 years old	59	23

TABLE 5.21

PERMISSIVENESS AND ALIENATION FROM CHURCH
BY WARM FAMILY RELIGIOUS IMAGES

	Difference	Proportion explained
Percentage point difference in alienation from church between those who are above the mean on permissiveness and those who are below the mean.	+16%	
Taking into account the effect of warm religious images	+ 8%	.50

TABLE 5.22

RELIGIOUS IMAGERY AND RELIGIOUS DEVOTION
IN BOTH CATHOLIC MARRIAGES

(Percent respondent high on religious devotion)

Images warm	Not warm
45*	27

*Significantly different from not warm.

TABLE 5.23

RELIGIOUS IMAGERY, RELIGIOUS DEVOTION AND SPOUSES
RELIGIOUS DEVOTION IN BOTH CATHOLIC MARRIAGES

(Percent respondent high on religious devotion scale)

	Images warm	Not warm
Spouse low devotion . . .	19	14
Spouse high in devotion .	78**	58

**Significantly different from those whose images are not warm.

TABLE 5.24

ALIENATION FROM THE CHURCH AND
FAMILY RELIGIOUS IMAGERY

(Percent not alienated)

Imagery warm   Not warm

32*   19

        *Significantly different
from not warm

TABLE 5.25

ALIENATION FROM THE CHURCH RELIGIOUS IMAGERY
AND SEXUAL PERMISSIVENESS

(Percent not alienated)

	Permissiveness	
	High	Low
Warm images	26	44
Not warm images	4	27[**]

[**]Significantly different from low permissiveness.

TABLE 5.26

PERMISSIVENESS AND RELIGIOUS IMAGERY
(Percent high on permissiveness)

Images warm	Images not warm
57*	84

*Significantly different from "not warm."

TABLE 5.27

ATTITUDES TOWARDS SEXUAL ISSUES BY RELIGIOUS IMAGERY
(Percent)

	Images warm	Not warm
Percent living together almost always or always wrong	43*	17
Percent birth control wrong	6	2

*Significantly different from "not warm."

TABLE 5.28

CORRELATIONS FOR MIXED MARRIAGES

(Spouse not Catholic)

	(r)
Parents in mixed marriages	.15*
Years of Catholic schooling	.12*
Warm religious images	.10*
Parent relationship to each other close . .	.10*

TABLE 5A.1

AGE AND RELIGIOUS BEHAVIOR

(Percentages)

Religious behavior	18-21	22-24	25-27	28-30
Mass (nearly weekly)	46	35	24	32
Communion (monthly)	41	27	21	25
Prayer (several times a week) . .	58	53	52	57
Living together wrong	25	15	25	29
Close (Z Score)				
God	.04	-.07	.02	.06
Church	.24	-.01	-.15	-.07
Parish	.22	-.04	-.14	.00

Conclusion: There seems to be a religious trough in years from 22 to 27 with increase in religiousness in years after 28.

Change in closeness to God and parish over past five years as perceived by respondents (according to age) (+ = closer)				
God	.02	.21	.43	.53
Parish	-.55	-.48	-.15	.11

Conclusion: Younger three groups report drift from parish, oldest drift back; all are closer to God but biggest shift is in oldest. two groups. Hence we seem to be dealing with a mini-life-cycle rather than a cohort effect.

Analytical and pastoral questions par excellence: What facilitates relatively successful passage thru mini-life-cycle?

TABLE 5A.2

CHURCH ATTENDANCE BY CATHOLIC AGE COHORTS
(NORC GENERAL SOCIAL SURVEY)[a]

(Percentages)

Cohort	1949-51	1946-48	1943-45	1939-41
Age:				
22-23	33			
24-25	35	54		
26-27	29	46	54	
28-30	55	43	36	56
31-33		43	43	35
34-36			44	58
37-39				65

[a]Attendance two or three times a month or more.

One cannot find, however, in Table A.3 evidence of a similar life cycle crisis for Catholics who were born before 1949. Indeed Catholics who were born between 1939 and 1945 seem to have experienced a sharp dip (of more than 20 percentage points) in church attendance in their early thirties and then also to have rebounded as this decade of their life went on.

It may be then that there are two major "dips" or "U curves" in religious behavior for Catholics, one in the middle twenties and the other in the early thirties. We will only be able to confirm this possibility when we can follow the cohort presently turning thirty into the next five years of its life.

TABLE 5A.3

CATHOLIC EDUCATION AND THE MINI LIFE CYCLE

Age	Ten years of Catholic education or more	Less than ten years
A. Z score on "Catholicity" scale		
18-21	1.10	.18
22-24	.27	- .11
25-27	.15	- .33
28-30	.51	- .21
B. Correlations between years of education experience and "Catholicity"		
18-21	.28[a]	.07
22-24	.16[a]	.05
25-27	.16[a]	-.05
28-30	.35[a]	-.18[a]

[a]Statistically significant correlation at .05 level or better.

Conclusion: Those who have gone to Catholic schools go down less deeply into the irreligious trough of the middle twenties and rebound more dramatically. In the returning age segment the more the years of CCD the less likely the young person is to "return" suggesting perhaps a negative influence of their religious education at this time. The most powerful positive correlation, on the other hand, is with Catholic education precisely at this age segment, suggesting that there is a special payoff in Catholic education when the "drift" back to religion begins.

TABLE 5B.1

CORRELATIONS WITH "COLD"[a] IMAGE SCALE

Marital Satisfaction	-.15
Sexual Fulfillment	-.15
Family joyousness	-.10

[a]Both husband and wife high on scales composed Jesus as "distant" and Mary as "distant".

TABLE 5B.2

"COLD" RELIGIOUS IMAGERY BY DURATION OF MARRIAGE
(Husband and wife both high on cold scale)

(z scores)

0-1	-.10
2-3	.08
4-5	.02
6-8	-.06
9-10	-.26

TABLE 5B.3

EXPLANATIONS OF INCREASE IN MARITAL ADJUSTMENT BETWEEN 7-8 AND 8-9 YRS.
IN TERMS OF COMBINATION OF WARM AND COLD IMAGES

	Marital Satisfaction	Proportion Explained	Sexual Fulfillment	Proportion Unexplained
Raw difference	+25%		+19%	
Differences with images taken into account	+14%	.44	+ 7%	.63

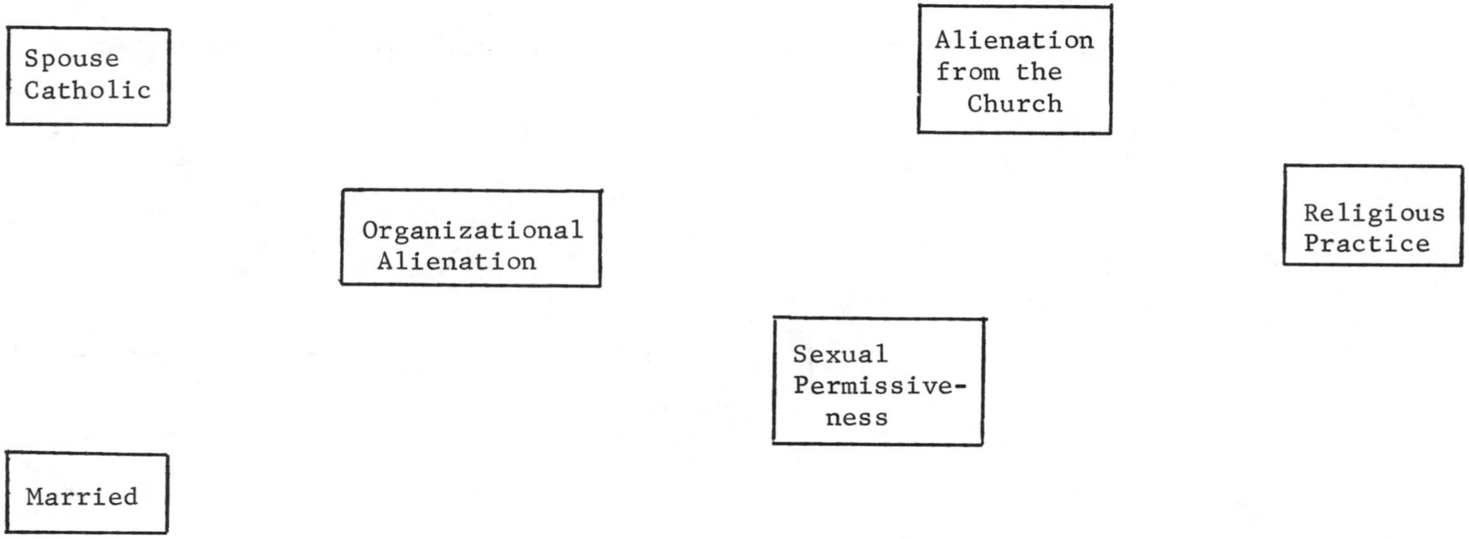

Fig. 5.1. Alienation model to explain religious life cycle in the twenties

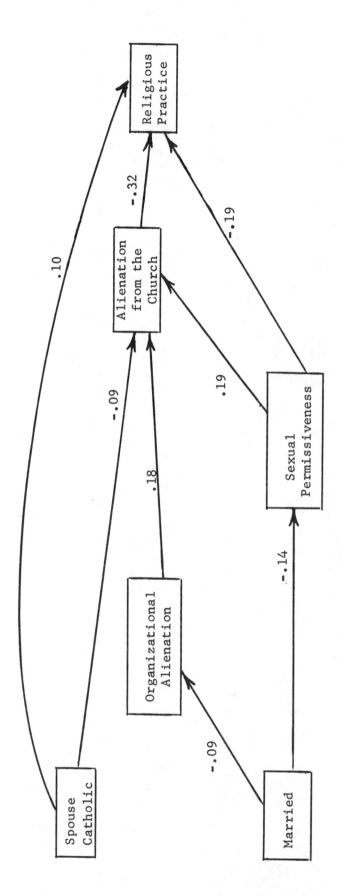

Fig. 5.2. Alienation model to explain religious life cycle in the twenties - USA

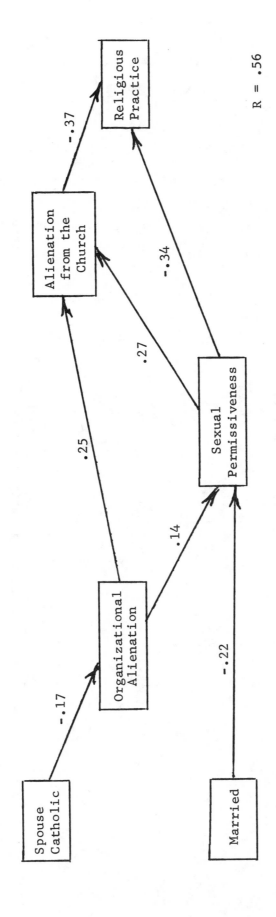

Fig. 5.3. Alienation model to explain religious life cycle in the twenties - Canada

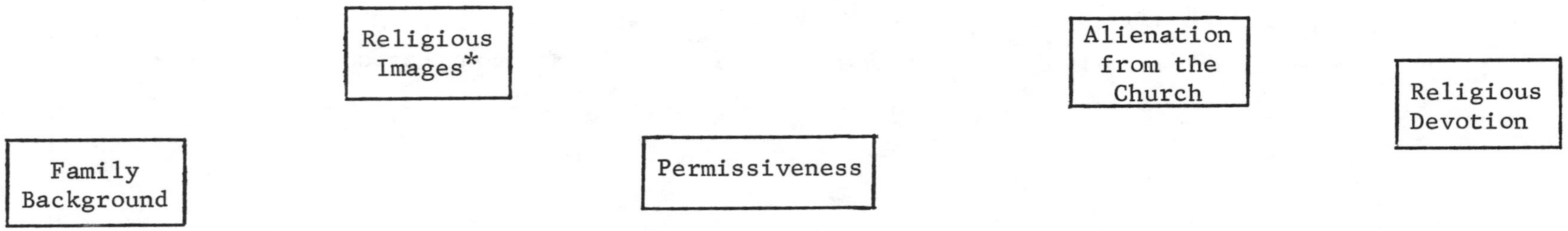

Religious Devotion

Alienation from the Church

Permissiveness

Religious Images*

Family Background

*Both spouses high on "warm" image scale.

Fig. 5.4. Model to explain why marriage improves level of religious devotion

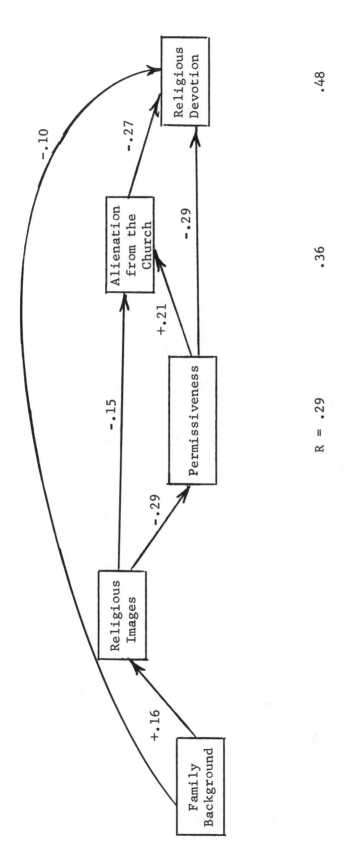

Fig. 5.5. Model to explain religious devotion in all marriages in which both partners are Catholic

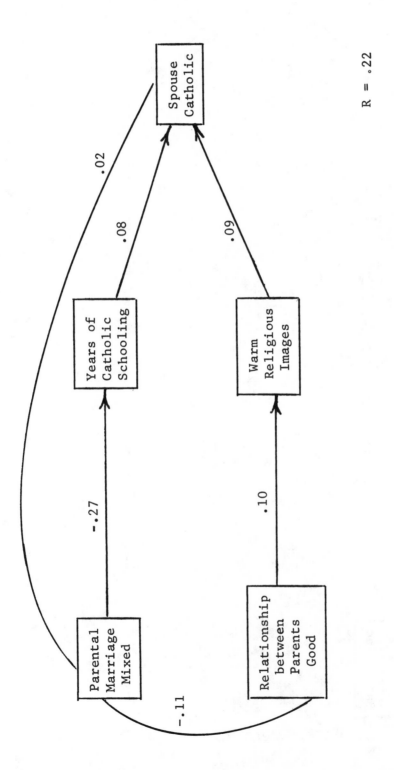

Fig. 5.6. Mixed marriages

TABLE 6.1

POLITICAL AFFILIATION AND DISAFFILIATION FOR
YOUNG CATHOLICS BY AGE COHORT

Age	Unaffiliated	Democrat	Republican
18-21	35	49	16
22-25	34	46	18
26-28	29	59	12
29-30	27	57	16

TABLE 6.2

POLITICAL AFFILIATION AND DISAFFILIATION BY SPOUSE'S
RELIGIOUSNESS FOR YOUTH CATHOLICS

Religiousness	Unaffiliated	Strong Democrats
Spouse very religious	13	18
Spouse religious	11	8
Spouse not religious at all	19	4

TABLE 6.3

CORRELATIONS BETWEEN SPOUSE'S COMMUNION
AND AFFILIATION

Affiliation	Correlation
Strong Democrat	.16*
Disaffiliated	-.12*

TABLE 6.4

POLITICAL AND SOCIAL CORRELATES WITH
"WARM RELIGIOUS IMAGES"

(Jesus "warm," Mary "warm," God "lover," heaven
paradise of pleasure and delights)

Religious Images	Correlation
Obligation to work for racial justice . . .	.11*
Should contribute to poor	.22*
(Important life goal:) Helping to solve social problems such as poverty and air pollution	.19*
Political disaffiliation	-.12*
Abortion (defect in child)	-.17*
Abortion (wants no more children)	-.39
Mercy killing	-.27*
Number of children	.03
Number of expected children	.08

TABLE 6.5

SOCIAL COMMITTMENT BY WARM IMAGE SCALE
(Percent high on social commitment)

Warm image score	
0 (low)	27 (157)
1	26 (173)
2	32 (218)
3	38 (147)
4 (high)	50 (32)

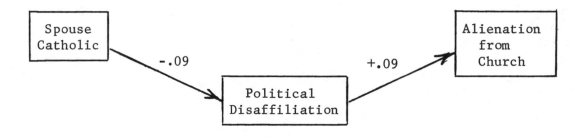

Fig. 6.1. Religion of spouse, political disaffiliation and
alienation from the church
(A fragment of the model in Fig. 5.2)

All Respondents

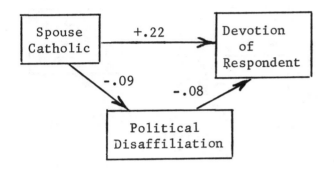

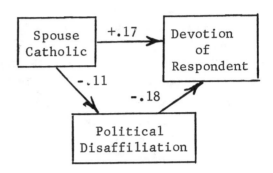

Fig. 6.2. Spouse's religion, political disaffiliation and respondent's
religious devotion

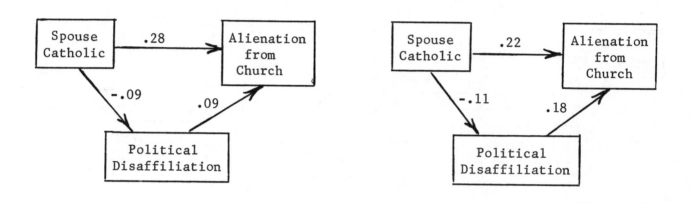

Fig. 6.3. Spouse's religion, alienation from the church, and political
disaffiliation

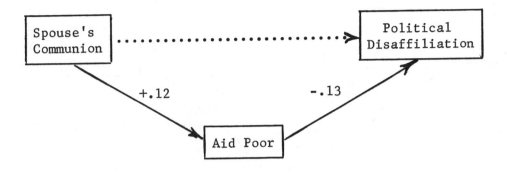

Fig. 6.4. Spouse's Communion reception, commitment to aid the
poor, and political disaffiliation

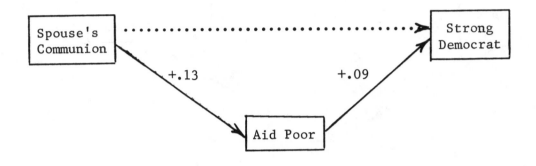

Fig. 6.5. Spouse's communion reception, commitment to aid the poor,
and strong Democratic affiliation

TABLE 7.1

CORRELATES OF WARM RELIGIOUS IMAGERY
(FOR INDIVIDUAL)

Religious Imagery	Correlation (r)
Family religious spirit[a]	.19
Religious experience[b] . ⚬	.18
Asceticism[c]	.17
Sermons	.25
Spouse's religiousness	⚬18

[a]Father and mother joyous in their approach to religion.

[b]In touch with higher power, sense purpose in life, in contact with the sacred (80% have at least one).

[c]Asceticism scale = talk to priest about religious problem, retreat, day of recollection, read spiritual book.

TABLE 7.2

CORRELATES OF HOPEFUL WORLD VIEW

Religious Imagery	Correlation
Warm religious images	.37
Family religious spirit . . .	.20
Religious experience	.26
Asceticism	.16
Sermons	.18
Spouse's religiousness . . .	.29

TABLE 7.3

CORRELATION BETWEEN RESPONDENTS' HOPEFUL WORLD VIEW
AND THAT OF SPOUSE'S BY LENGTH OF MARRIAGE

Length of Marriage	Correlation
1-2 years	.30
2-4 years	.33
5-6 years	.37
7-8 years	.60
9-10 years	.55

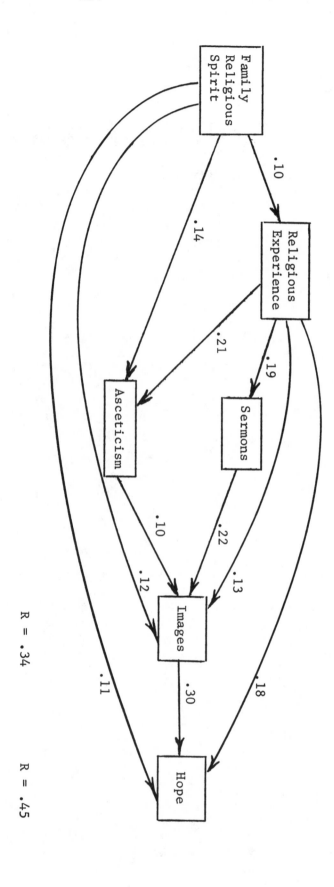

Fig. 7.1. Model to explain origins of warm religious imagery and hopeful world view

R = .34   R = .45

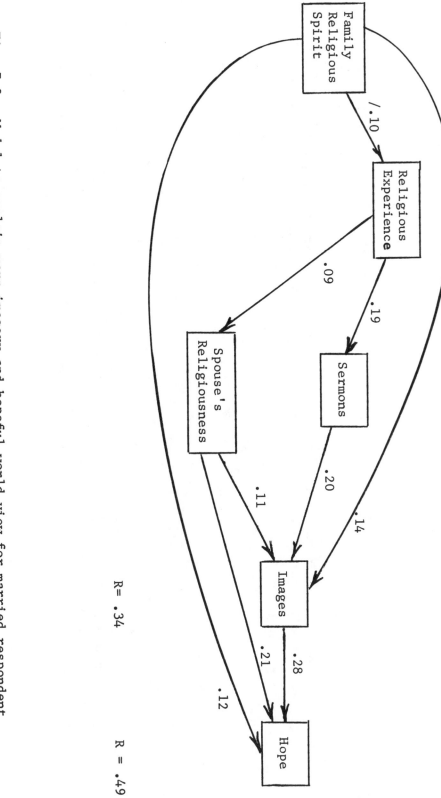

Fig. 7.2. Model to explain warm imagery and hopeful world view for married respondent

R= .34   R = .49

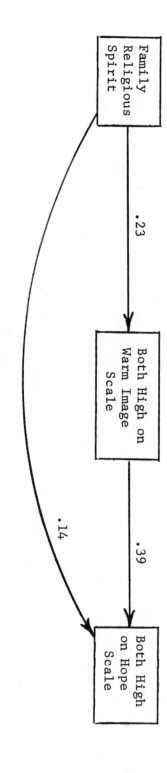

Fig. 7.3. Joint hopefulness (both husband and wife high on hopefulness scale) by joint religious imagery and religious spirit of family background of respondent

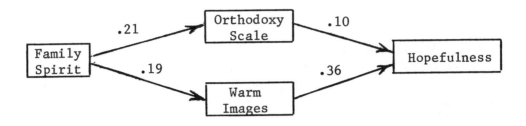

Fig. 7.4. Orthodoxy, images and hopefulness

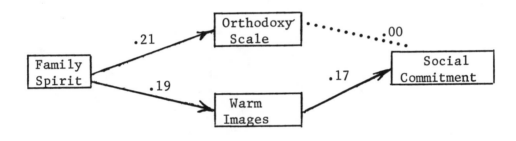

Fig. 7.5. Orthodoxy, images, and social commitment

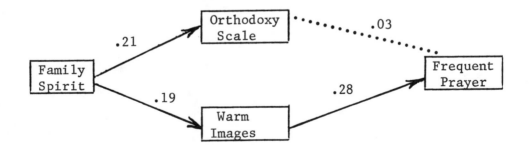

Fig. 7.6. Orthodoxy, images and prayer

TABLE 8.1

SEXUAL FULFILLMENT BY FAMILY PRAYER
(Percent both spouses report sexual fulfillment as
"excellent")

Both pray every day	One or other does not pray every day
42*	24

Gamma = .50.

*Statistically significant difference

TABLE 8.2

ASSOCIATION BETWEEN HUSBAND AND WIFE'S PRAYER
BY DURATION OF MARRIAGE
(gamma)

0-1 year	.31
3-8 years	.21
9-10 years	.42

TABLE 8.3

CORRELATIONS AMONG DAILY PRAYER, SEXUAL FULFILLMENT AND
WARM IMAGES
(All measures are family scores -- both husband and wife)

	Prayer	Sexual fulfillment
Sexual fulfillment	.20*	
Warm images	.19*	.26*

TABLE 8.4

SEXUAL FULFILLMENT BY DAILY PRAYER BY WARM IMAGES
(FAMILY MEASURES)
(Percent both excellent "sexual fulfillment")

		Both pray daily	
		Yes	No
Warm images	Yes	53*	27
	No	22	22

*Significantly different both in row and column

TABLE 8.5

DAILY PRAYER BY DURATION OF MARRIAGE
(Both husband and wife)

0-1 year	22
3-8 years	20
9-10 years	30

TABLE 8.6

PRAYER AND WARM IMAGES AS EXPLANATION FOR INCREASE IN
SEXUAL FULFILLMENT (BOTH SPOUSES) BETWEEN MIDDLE AND END OF
FIRST DECADE OF MARRIAGE

	Difference	Proportion of difference explained
Difference between 3-8 years and 9-10 years in percent of couples in which both spouses say sexual fulfillment is excellent	+22%	
Taking into account warm images of both spouses	+ 9%	.59
Taking into account whether both spouses pray every day	+ 6%	.73

TABLE 8.7

CORRELATIONS WITH ACKNOWLEDGED RELIGIOUS INFLUENCE OF SPOUSE

Both Warm Images	.23
Both Pray Daily	.23
Both Sexual Fulfillment	.16

TABLE 8.8

SPOUSE RELIGION INFLUENCE BY DURATION OF MARRIAGE
(z score)

1-2 years	+04
3-8 years	-02
9-10 years	+10

TABLE 8.9

RELATIONSHIP BETWEEN SPOUSE HAVING "VERY MUCH" RELIGIOUS INFLUENCE
ON RESPONDENT AND WARM IMAGES AND DAILY PRAYER BY LENGTH OF MARRIAGE

Warm Images and Spouse Influence	
1-2 Years	.57*
3-8 Years	.45*
9-10 Years	.65*

Prayer and Spouse Influence	
	.67*
	.24
	.58*

TABLE 8.10

PRAYER, SPOUSE INFLUENCE AND SEXUAL FULFILLMENT

	(Both Spouses High On Warm Images)	
	(% Both Say Sexual Fulfillment Excellent)	
	Both Pray Daily	One Or Both Do Not Pray Daily
"Very much influence by spouse	57% (14)	43% (14)
Not "very much" influence	47% (17)	21% (52)
Total	52 (31)	26 (52)
	(One Or Both Low On Warm Images)	
	36% (11)	*
	21% (88)	29% (14)
Total	22 (99)	22 (18)

*less than 5 cases

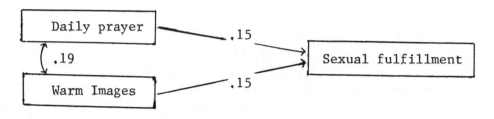

Figure 8.1. Standardized correlations (beta).

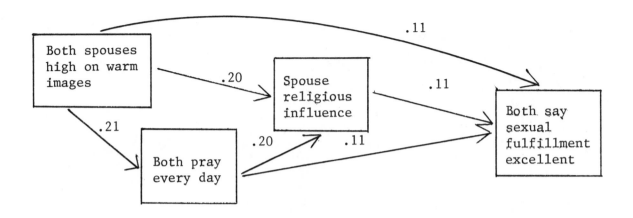

Figure 8.2.   Images, prayer, spouse influence and sexual fulfillment.